THE *Valley* OF
HEART'S DELIGHT

True Tales from Around the Bay

D1571769

ROBIN CHAPMAN

THE
History
PRESS

Published by The History Press
Charleston, SC
www.historypress.com

Front cover: Image of the Santa Clara Valley from the cover of a Sun-Kist sales book, 1916. *Courtesy History San José*; Vintage postcard of Esther Williams. *Author's collection.*
Back cover: Blossom Time in the Santa Clara Valley, promotional print from the California Prune and Apricot Growers Association, 1946. *Courtesy History San José.*

First published 2022

Manufactured in the United States

ISBN 9781467151474

Library of Congress Control Number: 2022935418

For my fellow LAHS Knights who have surrounded me with friendship for longer than I care to say.

CONTENTS

INTRODUCTION

*M*y great-great-grandmother Luthena Brumfield was in her farmhouse in Montana's Gallatin Valley one summer day about 1888, when she looked up to see a Crow Indian man wearing very little clothing standing in her doorway. Luthena's husband, a Civil War veteran, had recently died, and she was alone in the house caring for her eleven children, eight of whom were still in school.

"I don't know who was more frightened, him or me," she told a reporter in an interview recorded in Bozeman's *Big Timber Pioneer* in 1926. "I thought to grab the rifle over the fireplace, but truth be told I didn't know how to fire it."

Her second instinct was more practical. "He looked hungry. So, I reached for a loaf of bread I had been baking and handed it to him. He took it and went on his way." She later learned from a neighbor that the Crow man had only been looking for permission to water his horses.

Her daughter Rena, born in 1878, was my great-grandmother and may have been too young to remember what turned out to be a peaceful encounter that day between representatives of two civilizations in conflict. Rena Latta, as she became, lived long enough to marry; produce three sons; retire to Azusa, California; ride on the freeways of Los Angeles; and join our family on a trip to Disneyland when I was a child.

I learned the Luthena story from my grandmother Lena Latta on a visit I made to her home in Spokane, Washington, when I was a young reporter. She was a widow then, and I was working in the Pacific Northwest. She took the clipping about my great-great-grandmother's adventure from her scrapbook and gave it to me, and I still have it today, though it has grown battered in the intervening years.

On that same visit, my grandmother showed me a photograph of herself at thirteen wearing a spectacular hat and told me how she happened to buy it. She had been sent into town from her father's Montana farm with enough money to buy a hat and a dress for a family occasion. A sly salesgirl persuaded her to buy the hat, though it cost my grandmother all the money she had. She was too intimidated to say no. When she returned home in dismay, her father must

Lena Verwolf, who became my grandmother Lena Latta, in a circa 1908 photograph. She wears a spectacular hat and a sly smile. *Author's collection.*

have laughed, for he arranged to have her picture taken in her new chapeau. Among other things, I was relieved to know my attraction for accessories was not anomalous in my family.

These true stories of the West connect five generations—from my great-great-grandmother down to me, now writing in the twenty-first century. That is what our history does when we share it: it becomes a time machine that can move us through the centuries and bring us safely home again.

Like my maternal antecedents, I am a westerner. I grew up in California's Santa Clara Valley when it was in transition from its years as one of the most important centers for agricultural innovation in the world to its new role as a center for worldwide technological change. The fruit cooperative behind Sunsweet was founded in the Santa Clara Valley in 1917, and fifty-nine years later, the company Apple Computers was incorporated just up the road in the same valley. Today, along with millions of other people, I am a consumer of the products of both of these brands.

I grew up in this place and then spent many decades away from it in my work as a journalist. My parents, who built their first house in Los Altos, California, after World War II, stayed on. When I returned to care for them, I reconnected with my past. During the many years I had been coming home to visit, I had often sought out books on the valley's history at the local library and was surprised to discover there were so few of them. Perhaps history was changing so quickly in California it was difficult for historians to keep up.

After the deaths of my parents, I didn't plan to stay, but very soon found myself writing about this interesting place. There was a local man named Don McDonald who had been writing on local history for the *Los Altos Town Crier* then. Through his work as a volunteer at the Los Altos History Museum and my research in the museum's archives, I got to meet Don, and he turned out to have his own interesting story.

He grew up in Southern California and served as a naval officer in World War II. He then had a long career working around the world as a cryptographer for the NSA, the National Security Agency, a federal organization so secret its nickname was "No Such Agency."

After his wife died, he retired and moved to Los Altos for a reunion with a woman he had known in Los Angeles before World War II. They married and made their home in a charming cottage not far from downtown Los Altos. "Would you like some Rangpur limes?" he asked on one of my first visits. I didn't know what a Rangpur lime was, but on that winter day, he showed me a citrus tree in his garden so weighed down with them I could see why he needed to give them away. "They are great in a gin and tonic," he added, giving me his sparkling smile. Since I knew by then he had been stationed around the world in his work as a spy—I mean as a code breaker—I drew a picture of him in my mind, lounging on a veranda at sunset in some exotic clime, enjoying his quinine with gin and Rangpur juice.

He was a shrewd, congenial man and, by the time I got to know him, was in his nineties. I ended up writing a profile of him for a local publication for his ninety-sixth birthday. When he died a few years later, I not only missed his friendship, I also missed his well-researched work. Several years later, when I had completed work on a book, I approached Bruce Barton, editor of the *Los Altos Town Crier*, and asked if he would consider running a regular column from me on local history. He said he would be delighted. We called it "Santa Clara Valley Lives," which we hoped would allow the pieces to have a bit of range. The columns gave me the chance to continue the work begun by Don.

In the following pages, I've collected and combined forty-five different articles I first published in the *Los Altos Town Crier* and several other publications. I've woven the stories together not by their dates of publication or their dates in history but by their subject matter. The thread that

Lena Latta in Spokane, Washington, in the 1970s, wearing a scarf I had just given her. On this same visit, she gave me the news clipping about my double-great-grandmother. *Author's collection.*

connects them is the region—its people and their lives. I've also woven into them some of my own memories, as you will see. And, I've included the profile of Don McDonald in the last chapter about the lure of home. Don's story seemed a thoughtful bookend.

These short and rarely told tales are designed to be a diverting sampler in easily digestible bites of the flavors of the Valley of Heart's Delight— now the approximate locus of another mythical place known as Silicon Valley. As you will see, this valley surrounded by ocean and Bay has long featured diversity and innovation. I hope these tales will whet your appetite for further investigation.

The name Valley of Heart's Delight was once a marketing slogan, designed by the chamber of commerce to describe the orchard-covered Santa Clara Valley. Yet twenty-first-century residents have embraced this name as evocative of a place they love with a rich past and a thriving present. Many things have changed and many things remain, as these true tales will show. I like to think at least some of them would delight my grandmother, my great-grandmother and my otherwise unflappable great-great-grandmother, all of whom made the telling of these stories possible.

Chapter 1
APRICOT DAYS

My parents moved from San Francisco to Mountain View when I was five....
Silicon Valley for the most part at that time was still orchards—apricot orchards
and prune orchards—and it was really paradise.
—Steve Jobs

APRICOTS IN PARADISE

Charles Olson has been taking care of the apricot trees on the land that became Orchard Heritage Park in Sunnyvale for more than forty years. His fragrant fruit is so tempting, he often fields calls from residents who want to plant apricot trees in their own gardens, hoping their trees will turn out to be as beautiful and fruitful as his. One day, not long ago, Olson ordered fifteen apricot seedlings for a valley resident, which arrived just in time for spring planting.

Olson agrees that planting apricot trees is a wonderful gardening idea. In the mild climate around San Francisco Bay, apricot trees can survive on limited irrigation and, in all seasons, serve as distinctive California landscaping. And that's just for starters. One good apricot tree can produce two hundred pounds of fruit during the summer, and this can be eaten fresh or preserved for winter use. Still, even an amateur grower will have to work at it.

"You can't just plant 'em and walk away," says Olson.

Spanish missionaries brought the first apricot trees to the region. Father Junípero Serra, who headed the chain of missions in what became

Charles Olson wearing his trademark overalls at Sunnyvale's Orchard Heritage Park. *Photo by Robin Chapman.*

California, was born on the Island of Mallorca, where apricots—introduced there by invaders from North Africa—have been grown for centuries. The first Spanish immigrants to California discovered that the apricot, difficult to grow in many places, thrived in the rich soil and sunny weather of the Bay Area. British explorer George Vancouver, mapping the west coast of North America, saw productive apricot trees in orchards at both Mission Santa Clara and Mission San José as early as 1792.

In an interview published in 1892, an Ohlone man named Lorenzo said his father told him he recalled seeing the first fruit trees arrive at Mission Santa Cruz. "The trees were brought to the mission very small, in barrels," he told an interviewer, "so that the roots were kept damp. My father told me they had been brought from New Spain." New Spain was the name of Mexico then; the Spanish had been importing their culture—and apparently their fruit trees—to that region since the sixteenth century.

These first small orchards produced seasonal fruit for the missions, important because ships from the south arrived just once or twice a year with supplies. These first California immigrants had to produce or gather all their own food. It isn't surprising they would plant things they knew from home—whether their original homes had been in Spain or the lands beyond.

It wasn't until the Gold Rush that anybody thought about turning the trees into profit. Gold fever brought hundreds of thousands of miners to a region that for eighty years had been home to hundreds of thousands of Indigenous people but just a few thousand immigrants. There had never

The First Farmers, a woodcut by Franz Geritz, shows Franciscan fathers planting orchard trees. The print graced the cover of a California Historical Association publication in the 1930s. *Author's collection*.

been any commercial agriculture in California that could feed nearly half a million hungry newcomers. As the University of California's Edward J. Wickson wrote in 1914, "After the incoming of the Americans in 1849, some of the old Mission trees were secured by enterprising men...that they might minister to the great demand for fruit which sprang up among the gold seekers." These "enterprising men" took the fruit from the Bay Area missions and sold it in San Francisco, where it made them a profit and gave them the larger idea to become California's first growers.

The Spanish-speaking immigrants had been ranchers, not growers, and they found these Americans, with all their enterprise, annoying. Pío Pico, the last of the Mexican governors of California, complained about these "hordes of Yankees" whom he called "perfidious people" and who always seemed to be "cultivating" something.

And cultivate they did.

The opening of the transcontinental railroad in 1869 made it possible to ship California fruit anywhere. The commercial development of canneries during the Civil War led to the construction of at least sixty canneries in the valley. These industrial improvements gave early growers products they could ship by rail and steamboat to market. The commercial development of sun drying gave the valley another product that could safely be shipped. California apricots and other fruits became known around the world.

Many well-known residents became growers. John C. Frémont grew apricots on his land in San Jose. Sarah Winchester grew apricots and prunes on her 160-acre property. Valley pioneer Juana Briones, born in California to immigrants from Spain and Mexico, grew apricots too. From 1870 to 1970, orchards filled the Santa Clara Valley. With twenty-four thousand independent growers on 200,000 acres, orchardists became entrepreneurs—the forerunners, in spirit, of the innovators who invented Silicon Valley.

It was a business, but a beautiful one, giving the region blossoms in the spring, shade in the summer, green space, cash crops and scented fruit on the summer breeze.

Apple Inc. co-founder Steve Jobs, born in 1955, recalled in a 1995 interview what he liked best about growing up in the region: "Silicon Valley for the most part at that time was still orchards—apricot orchards and prune orchards," he said, "and it was really paradise." In 1997, when Jobs purchased the house next door to his home in Palo Alto and filed for permission to demolish it, it was not because he wanted a bigger house. He planned to fill the extra lot with apricot trees.

Orchards are not technically gardens, since they are agricultural acreage, but Charles Olson makes his orchard look like one. *Photo by Robin Chapman.*

Which brings us back to the apricot trees you might want to plant in your garden. Charles Olson of Sunnyvale says do it. But first, he suggests buying a book or checking one out from the local library on how to grow them.

"Good farming practices, I always encourage that," says Olson, a third-generation grower. Then he quotes an adage from his father: "Take care of your fruit trees, and they will take care of you."

OLSON AND A FAMOUS FRIEND

In his 1923 book, *Rural California*, Berkeley professor Edward J. Wickson wrote that as of 1920, there were 11,829,832 prune trees in California, 10,708,395 peach trees, 2,276,406 apricot trees and 750,794 cherry trees.

All stone fruits; all imported; and all thriving. A few years later, at the peak of the industry, there were 9 million apricot trees in the Santa Clara Valley.

Modern grower Charles J. Olson is one of the last of his kind in Santa Clara County. Born in 1935, he stands six feet, four inches tall. He played football at the University of Denver and then professionally in the Canadian Football League. He still lifts weights every morning, though his life no longer requires any heavy lifting. His family holdings, including a shopping center where an orchard once stood, have left him prosperous. You might think he's due for a rest. But he still cultivates an apricot orchard on twelve acres in Sunnyvale.

The trees stand on the remains of a thirty-acre parcel once owned by several other local entrepreneurs. The present orchard, long cultivated by Olson, is now Sunnyvale's Orchard Heritage Park.

"I've been tending these trees for almost half my life," he says. "Why quit now?"

Olson can nearly always be spotted wearing his trademark overalls, which look like a cross between Winston Churchill's World War II siren suit and a very large onesie. When I first wrote this description of him, he confessed he did not know what a onesie was, but after doing his due diligence and upon reflection, he decided the description was okay. In fact, the discussion of his overalls as unusual attire in what is now called Silicon Valley reminded him of a story.

He was in his orchard one summer evening back in the twentieth century—wearing his trademark overalls—when he saw a Lincoln Town Car with a chauffeur at the wheel pull up in front of his property. A square-jawed man emerged wearing clothing that seemed a bit dressy for Silicon Valley: a navy blazer, tan slacks, a button-down shirt and expensive loafers. The man introduced himself as Dave Packard.

"I just wanted to come down here and meet the crazy fool who was still farming in downtown Sunnyvale," said the co-founder of Hewlett-Packard, who confessed he himself had more than thirty acres of apricot trees in the hills above the valley.

The two men became friends.

Olson loaned equipment to Packard when he needed it. And one year, when Olson had a very small crop of apricots and needed more fruit, he called his friend Dave and asked if he could buy some fresh apricots from the billionaire.

Packard started laughing. Olson asked him what was so darned funny.

Dave Packard, one of the founders of Hewlett-Packard, had lots of famous friends, including Charles J. Olson of Sunnyvale and Queen Elizabeth II of Great Britain. Here, in 1983, he gives the queen a tour of an HP facility in Cupertino. *Courtesy Palo Alto Historical Association.*

The Packard apricot orchard in Los Altos Hills is not irrigated for practical reasons, says Mike McKinney, its orchardist. "It makes the fruit small," he says, "but very sweet." *Photo by Robin Chapman.*

"He told me he grew the apricots because he loved them and that driving the tractor gave him pleasure after a long day. He mostly gave his fruit away, he said, to his employees. He was laughing because I was the first guy who ever did that—offered him a profit on his fruit trees."

Dave Packard died in 1996 and deeded his orchard off Elena Road in Los Altos Hills to his family foundation to be cared for as a sort of apricot preserve. Olson's orchard also became a legacy when the plot of land he had been leasing for many years was designated as Sunnyvale's Orchard Heritage Park. It joined Saratoga's Central Park Heritage Orchard and the Los Altos Heritage Orchard as official landmarks to the visionaries who pioneered the first innovative business of the valley—the largest commercial fruit business the world had ever seen. Tech pioneers like Dave Packard and Steve Jobs raised their own fruit trees for pleasure as they nurtured their innovative companies in the valley.

"We have a great crop this year," said Olson, surveying the orchard. His fresh Blenheims go on sale each June, and he is among the many who believe there is no fruit as good as a tree-ripened apricot.

Eat them as often as you can if you want to make friends with innovators, like Dave Packard, or stay forever young, like Charlie Olson.

SUPERIOR FRUIT

People make a lot of money today in the region, and it is a good thing they do, with real estate values and property taxes among the highest in the nation. That's why this next apricot tale may challenge modern credulity. But it is an absolutely true story. I know this because the man who related it to me, Frank White, is a longtime family friend.

White is a businessman whose family moved to Los Altos in 1945. His father had been a fruit broker in San Francisco and, because of his job, spent a lot of time in the Santa Clara Valley meeting with growers and evaluating their harvests. He grew to love the sunny landscape south of San Francisco.

When World War II ended and Frank's father changed jobs, he made another change as well. He found a house on Covington Road in Los Altos, between El Monte Avenue and what is now Campbell Avenue. Built in 1928 as part of an enterprise called Costello Acres, the home had been designed to be a summer getaway for fog-bound residents of San Francisco. By the end of World War II, Costello Acres had become a neighborhood in the

Frank White, in 1946, in front of the family car and his childhood home. Over Frank's right shoulder, you can see a glimpse of the red-tiled roof of the house and beyond that a large apricot orchard, where Covington School now stands. *Courtesy Frank White.*

unincorporated village of Los Altos. The house sat on half an acre and was landscaped with twenty-two Blenheim apricot trees.

That number of mature apricot trees can produce as much as a ton of fruit each summer, and Frank's father knew the fruit had value. When the apricots ripened that first year, Frank, age eleven, and his father put on their work clothes, got out their ladders and picked the fruit, packing the apricots into wooden boxes called lugs.

Blenheims are one of the sweetest of the apricot varieties but are rarely grown commercially today because they don't travel well. Bump them and they bruise. To keep them from getting damaged in transit, the White family sealed the tops of the lugs with thin pieces of plywood and wrote their contact information on the top.

Then, they removed the back seat from the old family Packard, piled the lugs in the back of the car, drove to the railroad station in Mountain View and sent the fruit on the train to the produce market in San Francisco. The message came back from the buyers: "Superior fruit. Will buy all you have."

The apricot season is so short, growers say the fruit is "Green yesterday. Ripe today. Rotten tomorrow." Working against such a deadline, the Whites worked hard at their harvest, making many trips to the station during the next days and weeks, since each tree must be picked over and over again as the fruit ripens in its turn. When the season came to an end and their trees were picked out, the fruit that was rotten had to be buried in the orchard, one of the last jobs of the summer, but necessary to keep down the pests.

The family had earned a check for $101 on the sale of their apricots. The Whites had a home they loved, and the apricot trees on their land had rewarded them for their labor.

"The property taxes that year on my dad's house were ninety-eight dollars," recalls Frank, who now, instead of picking fruit, plays tennis three days a week to stay fit. "Our apricots paid the taxes and left us a little in change."

The house, by the way, is still in the family.

APRICOT COLORS IN OUR CALIFORNIA GARDENS

In the early years of immigrant settlement in California, newcomers who headed into the Santa Clara Valley found themselves astonished by its beauty. Franciscan friar Pedro Font walked into the valley in 1776 with Captain Juan Bautista de Anza and wrote in his journal: "The land is moist and the hills have an abundance of rosemary and herbs, sunflowers in bloom, vines as plentiful as a vineyard."

The hillsides seemed to be on fire. When the Spanish realized they were looking at acres of orange-colored wildflowers, they named the flower Copa de Oro, or Cup of Gold. It was given the botanical name *Eschscholtzia californica*, though you are more likely to know it as the California poppy.

"It is difficult to exaggerate the charms of this wonderful flower," wrote botanist Mary Elizabeth Parsons in her 1897 book, *The Wild Flowers of California*. "It revels in the sunshine." The Indigenous people liked to boil it or roast it on hot rocks and then eat it in a salad. Pioneers used an infusion of California poppy seeds as a mild substitute for morphine and a remedy for headaches. The Spanish fried it, added perfume and used the mixture on their hair.

California also has a wild peony and four different kinds of native roses. Other new plants the Europeans encountered were less benign. One, from the *sumac* family, was used by local Indigenous people for framing baskets and for barbecue spits. The Spanish, however, learned to avoid it, discovering *Rhus diversiloba* brought on a nasty rash, which is why today we call it poison oak. California's coastal tribes seemed immune to the rash, but that may be because the plant actually does not contain poison. Instead, it contains an allergen, and Indigenous people in the region may not have been allergic to it, as scientist Edward K. Balls noted, or "the plant could not have had so many uses in their everyday lives."

Other California wildflowers encountered by newcomers included three kinds of *Nicotiana tabacum* or Indian tobacco, so named because it was smoked by northern Indigenous people in some ceremonies. California also has a native *Apocynum cannabinum*, commonly called Indian hemp. Although it was used mostly for ropes, lariats, fishing nets and mats, a report from the nineteenth century also discreetly mentions, "A tincture made from the root is a recognized drug in the pharmacopoeia."

The Spanish brought their own gifts to our ecology. Gardeners will immediately recognize *Avena barbata* for its annoying way of popping up in every manicured flowerbed. It has a tall green stalk and a purple awn, fading in summer to the color of wheat, suggesting its common name—Spanish oats. It is believed the padres brought the seeds from Europe and scattered them throughout California as fodder for their cattle. Like many transplants, it has taken root and refused to leave.

From such rich choices, it was botanist Sara Plummer Lemmon of Oakland who urged the legislature in 1890 to adopt the golden poppy as our state flower, which became official in 1903. It had the beauty of its striking color going for it, sharing its hue with the apricot.

Though rumors abound that it is illegal to pick the California poppy, in truth, state law does not single them out but prohibits the taking of anything from property that

Writing about the California poppy in 1897, botanist Mary Elizabeth Parsons said it "revels in the sunshine." It has been the California state flower since 1903. *Photo by Robin Chapman.*

is not your own. That is based on an ancient law you may have heard about that prohibits stealing.

If you have California poppies in your garden, feel free to pick at will. You can always infuse them for a headache, boil them for hair oil or use them as a uniquely California garnish. Like poison oak, Spanish oats and our native *cannabinum*, they are living history in our California landscape. Just make sure you check with the Franchise Tax Board on that last botanical before cultivating, selling or lighting up.

A SIGN IN THE ORCHARD

There are very few commercial orchards operating today in the Valley of Heart's Delight, and most of those that remain are at its very southern end. Much of the soil is now covered with homes and apartments, fast-food outlets, office parks and other development. But as I've mentioned, there are three heritage orchards in the valley that preserve a living remnant of this region's agricultural past. And therein lies another tale.

The oldest one is the Los Altos Heritage Orchard on San Antonio Road, planted by J. Gilbert Smith on acreage he purchased shortly after the turn of the twentieth century. Smith built a house on the land as he nurtured his first trees. He completed the two-story frame home just in time for the 1906 San Francisco earthquake. His windmill fell down in the quake, but he counted himself lucky to have suffered only that.

His mother lived with him for many years, which may explain why he married his childhood sweetheart, Margaret Hill, so late in life—and then only after his mother died. As suburban life grew up around them, the Smiths continued to cultivate their 'cots for more than half a century. In 1954, Smith sold his orchard to the newly incorporated City of Los Altos for its civic buildings, and he negotiated quite a deal. He and Margaret would continue to live in their house on the property for the rest of their lives and would hold the fruit rights to all the apricot trees that were not removed for city buildings. The first city historian, Joseph Salameda, told the *Los Altos Town Crier* that the city promised the Smiths their apricot trees would only be cleared "as necessary." Smith, for his part, agreed that when he and his wife died, their house and the land under it would go to the city for a museum.

Smith continued to harvest his apricot crop until his death at the age of eighty-nine in 1966. His wife, Margaret, operated the orchard until her death in 1973. Remember Frank White and his family's superior fruit?

Cynthia Henderson Riordan paints the spring blossoms in the Los Altos Heritage Orchard, February 2014. At that point city hall had a sign, but the Heritage Orchard did not. *Photo by Robin Chapman.*

He recalls working for the Smiths picking and cutting apricots when he was young. When Frank ran into Mrs. Smith later in his life, he said she went home and returned with his timecard from the 1950s to show she remembered him, too.

After the Smiths were gone, city volunteers turned the Smith House into a museum, and Los Altos won a Santa Clara County Historical Heritage Award for Excellence in Historical Preservation. "The basis for making the award," wrote chairman Gail Woolley, "is your preserving of an early residence and apricot orchard and adapting the house as a history center. The Commission was impressed with the strong support demonstrated by your city in preserving a part of our valley's heritage."

In 1981, under the California Environmental Quality Act (CEQA), the Los Altos City Council voted to give the Smith House and the adjacent Heritage Orchard new status as City Historic Landmarks. Under CEQA, places of historical importance are among the features of the environment worth protecting.

The city of Saratoga, California, purchased one of the last working orchards within its city limits to preserve it as its Central Park Heritage Orchard. *Photo by Robin Chapman.*

By the 1980s, the orchards of the valley were vanishing. One huge cherry operation along Homestead Road in Cupertino became the Kaiser Permanente Santa Clara Medical Center. In the late 1970s, grower Burrell Leonard and several other orchardists turned their property into the shopping center Vallco Park.

Both Sunnyvale and Saratoga established heritage orchard landmarks, and both communities marked these orchards with signs.

For many years, Los Altos, which had the very first heritage orchard in the valley, never got around to putting up a sign nor posting the City Historic Landmark plaque. As long as the Los Altos Heritage Orchard did not have a sign, it was a threatened place, especially in a region where land is so valuable and historic memory so short. In the early twenty-first century, a group of neighbors grew concerned that the orchard's history would be lost if it was not designated with some kind of marker. I joined those who were working on this. To lobby for a sign, we needed to know more about the legal history of the space, and for a long time, we had a hard time finding it.

We had been trying to find a map of the Heritage Orchard's boundaries for quite a few years, as well as the documentation for its designation, when a neighbor and I were visiting the Los Altos History Museum one day, speaking with a woman there. In the course of our meeting, we happened to ask her a couple of questions about the Heritage Orchard.

"Let me see," she said, reaching for a black three-ring binder in a nearby bookshelf. "Oh, here you go," she said, flipping through a few pages.

Our eyes grew wide. There, inside this plain binder, was a map of the boundaries of the Los Altos Heritage Orchard, established by law in 1981. That was a big find. But there was more. Alongside the map, there were documents dating back to the 1950s, describing the city's unique relationship with this space.

The binder was assembled by Lee Lynch, chair of the Los Altos Historical Commission in the early twenty-first century, who pulled it all together with the help of volunteers before her death in 2007. She was worried about a city plan that proposed construction of new city buildings on the Heritage Orchard site. She donated the binder containing her research to the Los Altos History Museum, and it went into a basement bookcase there.

Like the purloined letter in the Edgar Allan Poe story, there the information sat for many years, hiding in plain sight.

Once rediscovered, the documents made it possible to brief everyone on the protected status of the Heritage Orchard, its legal size and its designation as a City Historic Landmark under CEQA.

Also in the file was a news clipping dated October 4, 2000, featuring local historian Don McDonald and headlined: "Purchase agreement with Gilbert Smith was to keep apricot orchard in perpetuity according to Don McDonald." McDonald, the former NSA cryptographer, arranged with a local reporter to do his interview in the Heritage Orchard, where he was photographed taking his stand for the trees in the middle of the stand of trees—a coded message for future generations.

Along the way to finding this cache, there were some turning points. Local businesswoman Catherine Nunes, using a Granicus search, uncovered a Heritage Orchard Maintenance Plan, commissioned by the city in 2006 but apparently mislaid. When one city official read the orchard needed a better irrigation system, he was surprised. "I thought we were dry-farming that land," he said. He was right. But it had not been the plan. Irrigation resumed, and the orchard brightened up considerably.

Through the years, many residents worked to save the Heritage Orchard and spoke up for a landmark sign. Among them was the late Al Galedridge,

It took almost forty years for the Los Altos Heritage Orchard to get this sign. When it was installed in June 2019, this photo ran in the local paper. But that did not seem a big enough celebration. *Photo by Robin Chapman.*

a well-known World War II veteran and local barber, who said he had helped to keep the orchard pruned back in the 1960s when so many of his clients stopped cutting their hair and he had plenty of free time to exercise his talent for trimming.

It is impossible to name all those who helped. But the one who perhaps deserves the most credit is the late Lee Lynch. Her legacy in that three-ring binder was of incalculable value.

In 2019, with the help of the Los Altos History Museum, the orchard's sign was designed and finally installed that summer. Neighbors, feeling it had indeed been a group effort, set aside a time to meet in the orchard and pose for a group photograph for the local newspaper as a way to celebrate. News editor Bruce Barton of the *Los Altos Town Crier*, figuring it might involve perhaps one city official and a couple of activists, expected to take a quick cellphone picture. Planning ahead, the group asked a neighbor to bring along her camera with a wide-angle lens. Someone else brought a stepladder, just in case a high angle was needed to include a crowd.

It was. Nearly one hundred people turned out. There were so many people that, even with the ladder and the lens, it was still tough to get everybody into the shot.

As the late summer sun set over the Los Altos Heritage Orchard, it darkened the outline of the distant Coast Range and shone into the eyes of the crowd. "Ready for the picture?" said a voice behind the camera. "You bet!" said someone else. Right on cue, everybody said, "Apricot!" And smiled.

The sign's photo op day, July 12, 2019. *Town Crier* editor Bruce Barton is at left, scrunching down and laughing, having already taken his photo. Orchardist Phil Doetsch is behind him in a T-shirt. I'm standing, the third person to the right of the sign (with my sunglasses atop my head). Council member Lynette Lee Eng sits under the word "Heritage" holding some apricots. *Author's collection.*

Chapter 2

FAMOUS FACES

To my friends in Los Altos, Gratefully.
—Bing Crosby

A CROONER KERFUFFLE

Harry Lillis "Bing" Crosby was perhaps the biggest multimedia star of the twentieth century. He had a band; he was a recording star; he had a hit radio program; he starred in movies. As radio faded and television ascended, he became a hit on television too.

In the book *Los Altos: Portrait of a Community*, assembled in 1999 by the late *Los Altos Town Crier* publisher Paul Nyberg and editor Bruce Barton, I read a small item next to the year 1959 that surprised me: "Bing Crosby pledges $10,000 for new Youth Center." Who knew about that story? I remembered going to teen dances at the Los Altos Youth Center, today known as LAYC. But I had never heard of Bing Crosby's involvement.

I discovered his connection to the project had faded for a reason.

Crosby, who died in 1977 at the age of seventy-four, was indeed one of the best-known American entertainers of his time. He was born in Tacoma, Washington, and raised in Spokane, and his singing talent made him an international celebrity at the very beginning of an era when wide distribution of records, radio and film made that possible. His 1942 recording of "White Christmas" remains one of America's best-selling recordings. Although he was never Hollywood handsome, he became a big movie star, winning an Oscar for his role as Father Charles "Chuck" O'Malley in the 1944 film *Going My Way*.

He also started the golf tournament that became the AT&T Pebble Beach Pro-Am, one of the most important tournaments in golf. And—though this is not nearly as well known—he quietly worked as a philanthropist in his later years, donating millions of dollars to youth centers and hospitals all over the country, especially in his adopted home state of California.

In 1959, Chris Wilder, the developer of the Rancho Shopping Center, led an effort to build a youth center in Los Altos and somehow secured a pledge of $10,000 from Crosby. The new building, which sits directly behind Los Altos City Hall, was completed in late 1960 at the cost of $97,000—quite a lot of money in those days—much of it paid for with donations that rolled in after the first big pledge from Crosby.

Bing Crosby, celebrated on this vintage postcard, was one of the biggest multimedia stars of the twentieth century. Very few people knew about his philanthropy. *Author's collection.*

The dedication ceremony was set for Sunday, January 15, 1961, and the region was abuzz when the *Los Altos Town Crier* reported in its January 11, 1961 edition that Crosby would be there. On January 12, the *Los Altos News* reported Larry Crosby—Bing's brother and sometime publicist—said the star would indeed attend and bring golfers Byron Nelson and Ken Venturi along with him. Bing was scheduled to be in Pebble Beach at about that time preparing for his tournament, set for January 19–22, 1961, so an appearance by Bing in Los Altos on January 15 did not seem far-fetched. Bing, by the way, would eventually buy a house in Hillsborough, twenty miles north of Los Altos. But that didn't happen until 1963.

Now, with his brother making the deal and the tournament scheduled for nearby Pebble Beach, how could the plan go wrong?

Students from Los Altos High School created a "Welcome Bing" sign, and the city commissioned a commemorative plaque to present to Crosby, designed by resident Warren Ferris, a calligrapher and consultant to the Library of Congress. On the big day, a group of local teens arrived for the dedication on horseback, anticipating the need for a good vantage point from which to see the stars.

James Thurber (no relation to the writer who created Walter Mitty) was mayor then, and his widow, Emily, is still an active resident. I tracked her

THURSDAY, JANUARY 12, 1961   (18 PAGES)   SINGLE COPY 10c

WELCOME BING—In preparation for der Bingle's arrival Sunday, this group of Los Altos High School seniors rolled up their sleeves and went to work. Among the many decorations arranged for the Youth Center dedication is this banner welcoming Bing Crosby, the popular singer-actor, who will be the featured guest. (Left to right) Charles Simpson, Donna Flynn, Bill Lee, Marylane Fitch, Jan Spence and Tom Hutchison.

Bomb Scare At Foothill

Foothill College students were evacuated from their classrooms early yesterday after a "bomb scare" telephone call to college receptionist, Bunny Shaw. Investigation proved the call a hoax.

The husky voiced prankster called at 9:30 a.m. and said, "There's a bomb in your building." Called out of a meeting after the scare, Business Manager George Castleberry said, "I personally felt it was a crank, but you always have to be on the safe side."

Detective John Neal of the Mountain View police department termed the prank a "federal offense" and said the FBI has been notified.

CITY DECISION DEFERRED

Expressway Path Strongly Opposed At L. A. Hearing

Should the Southern Pacific, Thomas Johannon,

Sunday Is The Big Day! Teen Center Dedication

By BUD STALLINGS

With the big day in the offing, Los Altos residents are excitedly buzzing over the coming of the world's most popular crooner—Bing Crosby.

The occasion, of course, will be the dedication of the newly constructed Los Altos Youth Center Sunday at 2:30 p.m.—and der Bingle is down for special guest honors.

Despite Bing's busy schedule, for he's right smack in the middle of his National Pro-Amateur Golf Tournament at Pebble Beach, the Academy-Award star has agreed to attend the dedication ceremonies.

And if that isn't enough, Bing informs us that he is bringing along Byron Nelson and Ken Venturi, renowned pro golfers. Other guests include trustees of the Crosby Championship Fund which contributed $10,000 and pledged another $5,000 towards the construction of the near-$100,000 Youth Center.

Impressive Program

Pre-program music will be provided by the Foothill College dance band with Milton Stocking directing. William T. Powell will serve as master of ceremonies.

Presentation of colors will be made by representatives of Scout Troop 38, Cub Pack 34, Explorer Ship 36 and Explorer Post 37. Girls of Troop 16 will lead the Pledge of Allegiance.

Invocation will be offered by Rev. James L. Spooncer, St. Simon's Catholic Church, followed by special choral selections by the Blach Junior High School Choir under the direction of Mary Alexander.

Chris Wilder, president of the Los Altos Foundation.

Rev. Charles Cox, pastor of the Los Altos Community Methodist Church and president of the Los Altos Ministerial Association.

Other Donations

The Los Altos Foundation, Inc., overseer of the construction of the Los Altos Youth Center, acknowledges gifts to the facility of materials and services totaling approximately $15,000.

President Chris Wilder says these contribute to the building's present estimated worth of $97,000.

These are contributors in the two categories as compiled by (Continued on Page 2)

Noted Artist Helps Prepare For Dedication

Artist Warren W. Ferris, 585

The weekly *Los Altos News* produced a big headline for its January 12, 1961 edition on the upcoming Youth Center dedication. Unfortunately, the guest of honor missed the party. *Photo by Robin Chapman.*

down to ask if she remembered the day Bing Crosby came to Los Altos with those famous golfers. She sounded very puzzled when I asked.

There is a reason she didn't remember. Though the Los Altos Youth Center was filled to overflowing that day for the dedication, and the students on horseback stood by, peering in the windows, Bing Crosby did not appear, and neither did the golfers. A photo in the next week's newspaper shows the unsmiling mayors of Los Altos and Los Altos Hills under the headline: "Mayors Show Crosby Plaque; Bing Not There to Receive It." This was the day Bing Crosby's name lost its star power in Los Altos.

Emily Thurber laughed when I told her. "Now I don't feel so bad," she said. "I was afraid I had forgotten. If he had been there, *then* I would have remembered."

And that's where the story ended. Or so I thought.

A Crooner Makes Good

After the story of Bing Crosby and the Los Altos Youth Center was published, I got a call from local resident Jim Shattock, born in 1954, who had recently returned to live in his family home in Los Altos after the death of his father.

In the summer of 1976—fifteen years after the Crosby no-show—Shattock had a job with the Los Altos Recreation Department, working while he waited to begin his training as a firefighter. Looking for something in a tool closet that summer at the Hillview Community Center—since demolished, but then not far from the Los Altos Youth Center—Shattock found a battered, framed photograph of Bing Crosby holding a plaque. It was on the floor of the closet and had been kicked around a bit. The glass covering the photo was smashed.

The funny thing is that Jim was less impressed with the signed photograph of the famous star than he was with the calligraphy on the plaque Bing Crosby was holding, which Shattock recognized as the work of his great-uncle Warren Ferris, who lived near his folks' home in Los Altos. He asked if he could take the photograph to show his mom. His supervisor, Jim Workman, said something like: "That old thing? Sure." Shattock took it home, showed his parents and then forgot about it. For forty-four years.

In 2020, he picked up the newspaper and read my story about Bing Crosby. He was sure the Bing photo must still be in his parents' home—the one on Arboleda Drive that he had just inherited upon the death of his 102-year-old father. "My mom and dad never threw anything away," he sighed.

Bing did receive his plaque, though when and where is not known. But the presentation was recorded in this photo, found fifteen years later at the bottom of a city utility closet. *Courtesy Jim Shattock.*

He began to sort through the stuff and found the old picture in one of the piles in a closet. It shows a tired-looking star, still in golfing togs, posing with his plaque. Stamped on the back is "Photo by Bill Early." Bing, it seems, did show up to receive his plaque—at some point—and did acknowledge it. We cannot be sure, but the photo appears to have been taken inside the Los Altos Youth Center. It is inscribed by Crosby: "To my friends in Los Altos. Gratefully, Bing Crosby." Did he arrange for the photographer? He must have arranged to sign the print and get it back to the city. We don't know whether it pleased the mayors or not. All we do know is that fifteen years later, this personally autographed photo turned up the worse for wear in a city tool closet.

Why Crosby missed the dedication is another mystery. There were no cellphones then, and since the event took place on a Sunday, all the city offices were closed. What could he have done had he been delayed? Whom might he have contacted, and how?

What we do know is that Bing Crosby did his best to make amends. And that was the act of a gracious star.

SWIMMING INTO WEDLOCK

A few years ago, I was reading an autobiography of the late movie star Esther Williams and found her book interesting for a couple of reasons. Williams was a long-legged swimming champion who became a movie star at MGM Studios beginning in the 1940s, and her book, *Million Dollar Mermaid* (Simon & Schuster, 1999), was written with co-author Digby Diehl, a man whose name I knew because he had been a journalism professor in my graduate program at UCLA. That's the first reason the book got my interest. But there was more.

Early in the book, Williams tells the story of her first marriage to Leonard Kovner and how she and Kovner came down one weekend in 1940 from San Francisco to Los Altos and got married at Christ Episcopal Church. As a Los Altos native, I had never heard this story, so I looked up Digby Diehl to see if I could call and ask him about it. I learned he had died in 2017. Esther Williams died in 2013. With both of them gone, it meant the two best sources on this story were definitely unavailable for interviews.

However, a marriage requires a license, so I drove to the Santa Clara County Hall of Records in San Jose to see if I could get a copy, and for a fee, I was able to do that. New privacy laws in California mean a lot of information is redacted when public records are requested by nonfamily members—even for a marriage that is eighty years in the past and in which all of the key participants are dead. The names of the witnesses, for example, had been excised, as had the names of the county officials who signed the document.

The license nevertheless does confirm the story and shows that on June 25, 1940, when it was issued, Williams was living at 25 Capra Way in San Francisco. Kovner gave his address as 232 San Jose Avenue, San Francisco— which may have been a rooming house or a small hotel, since in her book, Williams says Kovner, a pre-med student at Los Angeles City College, had just come up for the weekend. She was almost eighteen years old, and Kovner was twenty-one.

Williams was not yet a movie star and only a temporary resident of San Francisco herself. She was performing in something called Billy Rose's Aquacade, a feature of the Golden Gate International Exposition at Treasure Island. She was a champion swimmer and had qualified for the 1940 Summer Olympics. But the games were cancelled by the outbreak of World War II in Europe, and Williams took the job in San Francisco instead.

Coincidentally, as I worked on this story, I happened to read the memoirs of a woman who in 1940, as a ten-year-old refugee from Hitler, found herself in San Francisco staying with relatives. Young Phyllis Finkel left behind a Europe in crisis, and everything about peacetime San Francisco was magical to her, including the fair on Treasure Island, which she visited more than once. "Especially memorable was Billy Rose's Aquacade," she wrote, "as I watched wide-eyed the thrilling performance of Esther Williams diving into a pool through a ring of fire."

Esther Williams was indeed memorable, and her job with the Aquacade brought her a lot of attention as she appeared in a swimsuit for three shows each day. Not all of the attention was welcome. First, Billy Rose, the middle-aged producer of the show, who had previously been married to comedienne Fanny Brice and was then married to swimmer Eleanor Holm, tried to seduce Williams by calling her to a "meeting" one evening in his suite at the St. Francis Hotel. When she managed to block that pass, she faced constant harassment from co-star Johnny Weissmuller, an Olympic gold medalist, also a married man, best known for his movie role as Tarzan. In her book, Williams says Weissmuller, twenty years her senior, repeatedly stripped off his swimsuit and chased her around backstage.

Williams was young and thought a wedding ring might stop the harassment.

Esther Williams was one of MGM's biggest stars in the 1940s and 1950s. She had her first wedding in the Santa Clara Valley. *Author's collection.*

When her boyfriend, Leonard Kovner, came up from Los Angeles for a visit, the couple decided to elope. "This marriage would protect me," Williams wrote, "from those busy men with grasping hands."

We don't know how she chose Los Altos or Christ Episcopal Church—the marriage license identifies it as the Protestant Episcopal Church and redacts the name of the priest. In 1940, Christ Episcopal, now on University Avenue, was located at 461 Orange Avenue where Foothills Congregational Church now stands. Neither Williams nor Kovner had a car, so taking the train that day would have brought them to the local depot of the Southern Pacific Railroad, and the church was just across the street.

The couple honeymooned that weekend—though Williams does not say where. Then the groom returned to Los Angeles, and the bride went back to work. Within a year, Esther Williams had signed her first movie contract and had separated from Kovner, whom she found controlling and abusive. She married three more times, eventually having a long marriage to movie star Fernando Lamas—from 1969 until his death in 1982—which made her the stepmother of actor Lorenzo Lamas, who says she was very kind to him and taught him how to swim.

Esther Williams made her last film in 1963 and in the 1980s worked as an Olympic swimming commentator for ABC Sports. She died in 2013 at the age of ninety-one, leaving behind—younger and bereaved—Edward Bell, husband number four.

Briefly, her life touched the Santa Clara Valley, and here, for a few days, she found romance and a respite in the sunshine.

ALFRED HITCHCOCK AND *THE BIRDS*

Alfred Hitchcock was a rare director who became as famous as the movie stars he featured. His profile was so iconic, it was used in the opening of his hit anthology series, *Alfred Hitchcock Presents*, which ran on network television in several forms from 1955 to 1965.

What most people in Northern California don't know today is that for most of his life in the United States, Hitchcock had a country home in the foothills above the Santa Clara Valley and that living in the region had a definite impact on his work. In fact, the very real events of the night of August 18, 1961, not far from his home in the region, directly influenced the plot of *The Birds*, one of the most famous Hitchcock movies of all time.

Alfred Hitchcock displays his famous profile on the shaded patio of his Scotts Valley estate, a profile made famous in the opening credits of his popular television show. *Courtesy UC–Santa Cruz Special Collections & Archives and Tere Carrubba.*

Hitchcock was born in London in 1899 and after studying art and working in advertising began his film career in England during the days of silent movies. After the advent of sound, his work, including *The Man Who Knew Too Much* (1934), *The 39 Steps* (1935) and *The Lady Vanishes* (1938), gained worldwide acclaim. In 1939, he signed a contract with producer David O. Selznick, who was just completing *Gone With the Wind* (1939), a film that went on to win eight Academy Awards. Hitchcock, along with his wife and creative partner, Alma Reville, and their daughter, Patricia, moved to Hollywood.

His first film under the new contract was *Rebecca*, a movie based on a mystery by Daphne du Maurier, a best-selling book on both sides of the Atlantic and a tale so successful it is still in print. This first Hitchcock production in America starred Joan Fontaine in the lead as the unnamed heroine; Laurence Olivier as her husband, Max de Winter; and Judith Anderson as the evil Mrs. Danvers.

During the course of the production, the Hitchcocks became friends with Joan Fontaine's mother, Lillian—also the mother of Olivia de Havilland, who went on to win one of those Oscars for *Gone With the Wind*. Hitchcock told Lillian he was thinking about looking for a country home outside

Hollywood where he could keep horses and make wine, and Fontaine suggested he look in the foothills of the Santa Cruz Mountains just above her home in Saratoga, where the climate was known to be good for growing grapes. In the autumn of 1940, Hitchcock purchased the estate locally known as Heart o' the Mountains on two hundred acres near Scotts Valley in an unincorporated area of the foothills called Vine Hill. It was "their first American home," says biographer Patrick McGilligan, and a way to "celebrate their success" in the United States.

The Hitchcocks enlarged the home, hired a staff and spent many weekends there at a time when there was easy, overnight train service between Los Angeles and San Jose. And though the estate was designed as a retreat, Hitchcock and his wife were early adopters of the work-from-home ethos. When they were developing a script, which was most of the time, they liked to brainstorm with industry friends and co-workers at their home in Bel Air or their place in Scotts Valley. The couple worked and played on their Bay Area estate and entertained their growing group of Hollywood friends there, including Ingrid Bergman (who starred in three Hitchcock films), Cary Grant (who starred in four) and Robert Cummings (who starred in two), among many others. In an evocation of the cameos for which he became famous on screen, Hitchcock could sometimes be spotted by surprised locals as he shopped for antiques along Big Basin Way in Saratoga.

Now that we've set the scene, it is time to dissolve to the scary part.

Hitchcock was not in residence at Heart o' the Mountains on the night of August 18, 1961, when a strange event took place not far from his home along the Santa Cruz coast, but he seems to have heard about it almost immediately.

Residents of Capitola and nearby Aptos were asleep on that foggy night when, just after 3:00 a.m., they were awakened by the sounds of what reporter Wally Trabing called "a rain of birds, slamming against their homes." Thousands of sooty shearwaters—a kind of gull—gorged on anchovies and apparently confused in the fog, descended on the coast between Pleasure Point and Rio del Mar, crashing into windows and slamming into roofs, light poles and aerial TV antennas. They hit a power line and caused an outage. They smashed into Deputy Ed Cunningham's prowl car and left him with a broken spotlight and a dead bird hanging from the roof of his cruiser.

Eight residents were injured when they rushed outside and sustained bird bites. As dawn broke, the streets were littered with thousands of birds, both dead and alive.

Oscar winner Ingrid Bergman and Alfred Hitchcock on his estate. He's holding a small camera, and Bergman appears to be having fun posing. *Courtesy UC–Santa Cruz Special Collections & Archives and Tere Carrubba.*

Hitchcock was in Hollywood that week, developing his treatment for *The Birds*, a film loosely based on a Daphne du Maurier short story set in Cornwall. Though regional news wasn't always as quickly disseminated then as it is today, Hitchcock was alerted almost immediately and called the newsroom of the *Santa Cruz Sentinel* requesting a copy of its August 18, 1961 newspaper, which featured the front-page headline "Seabird Invasion Hits Coastal Homes." He made the call himself, which was then reported in the newspaper's August 21, 1961 edition under the headline: "Alfred Hitchcock Using *Sentinel*'s Seabird Story."

"Despite its obvious publicity benefits for his new picture," reported the paper, "Hitchcock denied having anything to do with the feathery invasion of Capitola. 'Merely a coincidence,' Hitchcock purred knowingly."

Research suggests this call was very much in character for Hitchcock the moviemaker, who kept abreast of news events and looked for any connection that might help him sell his ideas to the studios and to his audiences. Norman Lloyd, a talented character actor who died in 2021 at the age of 106, was a longtime Hitchcock friend. He played a villain in Hitchcock's *Saboteur* (1942) and recalled that when the French liner SS *Normandie* caught fire at the docks in New York during the making of that movie and sabotage was

A vintage postcard promotes Alfred Hitchcock's movie *The Birds*. *Author's collection.*

suspected, the director sent a newsreel crew to New York to capture the flames. Hitchcock was, said Lloyd, "really on his toes and aware of any opportunity to create something for his film: to take history at the moment and incorporate it into a script—in character, story and action."

A strange bird attack in the headlines near his home in Northern California as he developed a screenplay about a strange bird attack was just the kind of connection Hitchcock loved.

The Birds landed in theaters two years later and was a hit. Celebrated reviewer Judith Crist said it was "enough to make you kick the next pigeon you come across." John Stanley called it "spine tingling." Unlike the Daphne du Maurier story, the movie is set in a tiny California beach town, not far from San Francisco. And though it does feature several elements from du Maurier—including a dead farmer with his eyes pecked out by birds—it also owes a lot to the mysterious assault on Capitola. The movie exteriors, however, were shot in Bodega Bay, across the Golden Gate Bridge in Sonoma County.

And what of the Hitchcock home in the mountains? The family enjoyed it for many years, finally selling it in 1974 as Alfred and Alma Hitchcock spent less time entertaining.

The curious incident of the sooty shearwaters in the night has not been repeated along the California coast. Scientists speculate that the birds in the real incident may have been poisoned by a natural toxin in the anchovies. No one knows for certain.

Whatever the cause, it was a mess for Capitola. But it was a lucky break for Alfred Hitchcock. And for fans of movie mayhem everywhere.

A WRITER OF THE WEST

Wallace Stegner was a Santa Clara Valley resident who was a star in the world of literature, where his work won him a Pulitzer Prize for *Angle of Repose* (1972), a National Book Award for *The Spectator Bird* (1977) and many other honors. At Stanford University, Stegner founded the creative writing program and mentored writers Larry McMurtry, Ken Kesey, Thomas McGuane and Edward Abbey, among many others. Sandra Day O'Connor, the first woman to serve on the Supreme Court of the United States, was another of his students.

Though he came to the Santa Clara Valley from a teaching job at Harvard, Stegner was not an easterner. Born in Iowa in 1909, he spent most of his childhood moving through "twenty places in eight states and Canada," as he later wrote. His father repeatedly uprooted the family as he tried one get-rich-quick scheme after another. The son found success in school. He spent his high school years in Salt Lake City, where a scholarship helped him earn his undergraduate degree at the University of Utah.

Fellowships enabled him to get his master's degree and then a doctorate at the University of Iowa, a school that was developing one of the best creative writing programs in the country. It was in returning to his home state of Iowa, "which I then thought of as the East," he wrote, that he discovered he had been changed by the vistas of the American West.

"I was used to a dry clarity, a sharpness in the air," he wrote in an unpublished autobiography. "I was used to horizons that either lifted into

A photographic portrait of Wallace Stegner created shortly before he moved to California to teach at Stanford University. *Courtesy Special Collections, J. Willard Marriott Library, the University of Utah.*

jagged ranges or rimmed the geometrical circle of the flat world. I was used to seeing a long way. I was used to earth colors—tan, rusty red, toned white—and the endless green of Iowa offended me. I was used to a sun that came up over the mountains and went down behind the mountains. I missed the color and smell of sagebrush, and the sight of bare ground."

Beginning in 1938, Stegner attended the annual Bread Loaf Writers' Conference in Vermont and through his contacts there began teaching at Harvard University, where he and his wife, Mary, and their son, Page, spent most of the years of World War II. When he got the chance to teach at Stanford University, he and his family loaded up their car and headed to the West.

It was not an easy move. No civilian housing had been built in the San Francisco Bay Area during the war, so when they arrived at Stanford in 1945, the Stegners spent two years moving between rented rooms, rooming houses in Palo Alto and dormitories at Stanford. Mary Stegner, a committed socialist, urged her husband to join the Peninsula Housing Association, which was hoping to build a cooperative community adjacent to Portola Valley. But, says Stegner biographer Jackson Benson, "delays and disagreements gradually discouraged" the Stegners, and they left the association. That's when they found 2.4 acres on a hilltop off Page Mill Road and decided to build their home.

Stegner on the campus of Stanford University about 1945. *Courtesy Special Collections, J. Willard Marriott Library, the University of Utah.*

Even that was complicated. The property was in unincorporated Santa Clara County, so when they bought the property, it had no city services or utilities. There was no road to the lot, no water, no electricity, no sewer connection and no refuse pickup. Stegner figured he could only afford the home if he did much of the finishing work himself.

The result was markedly different from the homes being built in the region today. The Stegner house was 1,800 square feet, with just two bedrooms and two baths. Later, they added a one-bedroom cottage where Stegner could write and the occasional guest could stay. Designed in the modern, utilitarian style popularized in California by Joseph Eichler, the home suited the Stegners' needs, and they lived there for nearly half a century.

During those years, Stegner became a keen observer of the constant struggle in the West between development and conservation. As a westerner—albeit an adopted one—he knew it was never a simple thing, this tug-of-war. The subject was at the core of his novel *All the Little Live Things*, published in 1967

In 1947, Stegner joined Norman Nevills's expedition down the Colorado River. Nevills, famous for never flipping a boat or losing a customer, was killed two years later with his wife, Doris, in the crash of their light plane. Nevills is at far left, Stegner is rear, fifth from left and his wife is front, fifth from left. *Courtesy Special Collections, J. Willard Marriott Library, the University of Utah.*

and set in the Santa Clara Valley's foothills. As his character Joe Allston says, "I admire the natural, and I hate the miscalled improvements that spread like impetigo into the hills. But who can pretend that the natural and the idyllic are the same? The natural is often imperfect....So I clean it up and grub out its poison oak and spray for its insect pests and plant things that bear blossoms instead of burrs, and make it all Arcadian and delightful, and all I do is help jar loose a tax increase, bring on roads and power lines [and] stir up the real estate sharpies."

Stegner wrote every morning. which may explain his prolific output as he taught at Stanford for a quarter of a century. During his years there, he published eight novels, fourteen books of nonfiction and six collections of articles and stories.

Faith Bell, whose family owns Bell's Books in Palo Alto and who lives in the nearby Palo Alto foothills, told me she saw Stegner often, both in her store and on the trails above the valley. "We would nod to each other," she says. "But, especially in the store, we try not to disturb people if they want anonymity."

A portrait of Wallace Stegner in 1977 when he was sixty-eight years old and had just won the National Book Award. *Courtesy Special Collections, J. Willard Marriott Library, the University of Utah.*

Stegner retired from Stanford in 1971 but continued to write into his eighties. His last collection of work, *Where the Bluebird Sings to the Lemonade Springs*, was published in 1992, and he died the next year. After the death of his wife, Mary, his beloved home was sold. And though there was a campaign to preserve his writing studio, both his home and studio were eventually demolished.

He is today perhaps best known as a conservationist, and that is in part because of his tenure as a board member of the Sierra Club and his service to the Department of the Interior in the Kennedy administration. He is especially known for the Wilderness Letter, an impassioned plea he wrote in 1960. In it, he says, in part: "We need wilderness preserved—as much of it as is still left, and as many kinds—because it was the challenge against which our character as a people was formed." His eloquent words became part of the Wilderness Act of 1964.

If you hike the trails in the hills in the open space district above Stanford University, you might see a bench marked by a plaque, dedicated by his wife, Mary, after his death. There you will find Stegner's creed for the region he loved: "To try to save for everyone, for the hostile and the indifferent as well as the committed, some of the health that flows down across the green ridges from the Skyline, and some of the beauty and refreshment of spirit that are still available to any resident of the valley who has a moment, and the wit, to lift up his eyes unto the hills."

Chapter 3

OLD FRIENDS

The old fellow says when he was a little boy, his tribe was numerous about here,
but all have died and he is the only one left.
—Alfred Doten

O ne of the interesting things about writing history is that even after a book is published, the research continues. Publishing has deadlines; learning never ends.

For several of the lives I feature in the book *Historic Bay Area Visionaries*, this has proved true. In more than one of the stories that follow, new information and sometimes new mysteries have come to light.

A Photographic Mystery

Lope Inigo had his picture taken by a San Francisco photographer in 1856 when he was seventy-five years old. Studying his life, all of which was spent in the rural Santa Clara Valley thirty-seven miles south of what became the city of San Francisco, I began to think it was curious he sat for this photographic portrait when doing that was such a rare thing at that time.

He was born in an Indigenous village near what is today Mountain View in 1781, four years after the founding of Mission Santa Clara—essentially, in the early years of Spanish and Mexican immigration into California. When he was eight years old, his family brought him from their village to be baptized at the mission, just after Christmas in 1789. His life had begun at a time when his people, whom we now call the Ohlone, were living as their people had lived on the edge of San Francisco Bay for untold millennia. His life in California extended more than eight decades on into the age of the Industrial Revolution.

After he was baptized, he lived the first half of his life at the mission. A lot of what we know about him comes from the mission records. There he worked, there he married and there he became an *alcalde*, a civic official for his people. He was married at sixteen to a bride from another village. She had been baptized at Mission Santa Clara as Maria Viviana and was fifteen on her wedding day.

The couple were married for three decades until her death in an epidemic at the mission in the winter of 1827–28, which also took the life of their two-year-old son, José Tomas. The close-knit mission environment was terrible for the spread of disease. The Spanish had no understanding of this, and the Indigenous people at the missions had no immunity to European diseases. Epidemics killed 20 percent of the Mission Santa Clara population in 1802 and another 16 percent in 1806. Of Inigo and Viviana's eleven children, just three survived to become adults.

Since I first wrote about Inigo, I have learned that not everyone in the Americas was as lacking in understanding about epidemics as were the early immigrants to California. In 1777, George Washington ordered all his troops to be inoculated against smallpox using the live virus—called *variolation*—and that disease "largely disappeared from the ranks," says Pulitzer Prize–winning historian David Oshinsky. George Washington was himself a survivor of smallpox, and after inoculating his troops, his biographers say he also obtained quinine to help his soldiers fight malaria. The new immigrants to California were very isolated by geography and seem to have lacked knowledge of the growing research on these lifesaving scientific advances.

In California, the isolated missions were secularized between 1833 and 1836 and had to become self-supporting churches to survive. Inigo, by then a widower in his fifties, held the newly independent Mexican government to its promise of land and applied to obtain his own ranch. He sought the land of his ancestral village and did not give up when he faced delays.

In fact, he persisted for years, eventually moving to the land as a squatter in about 1838, since that was an agreed-upon strategy for staking a claim. By 1841, he had acquired livestock and his own brand for his cattle. In 1844, after Father Jesus María Vasquez del Mercado at Mission Santa Clara intervened, the penultimate Mexican governor of California, José Manuel

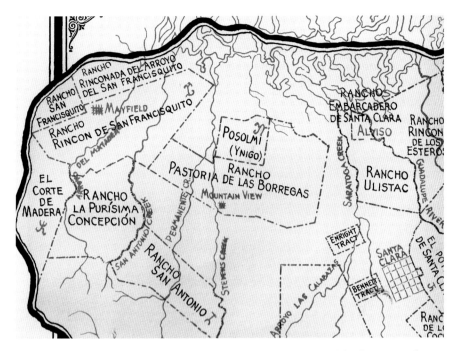

This map of a section of Santa Clara Valley's ranches shows three of the four properties granted by Mexico to Indigenous families in the valley. Rancho Posolmi was owned by Lope Inigo; Rancho Ulistac by Marcelo Pío; and Rancho La Purísima Concepción by José Ramón and José Gorgonio. *Courtesy History San José.*

Micheltorena, finally granted Inigo the 1,686 acres of what became Rancho Posolmi on land between the present-day city of Mountain View and San Francisco Bay. It was half the amount of acreage he had been promised; a Mexican official had stolen the other half for a relative.

In 1844, Inigo, a widower now sixty-three years old, married a young widow in a ceremony recorded at the mission. For the first time in his life, he had a home of his own to share with his family.

It turns out he won his ranch just in time. Five years after the grant was issued, the Gold Rush created a land boom as Americans from the East and people from all over the world—nearly half a million of them—came to California seeking their fortunes. In the 1852 U.S. Census, six of Inigo's family members are listed as living on his ranch, though there may have been others there who went unrecorded. His land was now increasingly valuable for privacy and protection.

Then, in 1856, Lope Inigo had his photograph taken. In those days before the Civil War, these expensive portraits were often for the prosperous. Inigo lived on a rural ranch that had just four buildings—two of wood and two of adobe—and the glimpses we have of him in that era suggest his life was rustic. A visitor reported seeing him in his home one afternoon weaving cloth at a loom. Another described stopping by his well and finding an Indian basket there used for drawing water. It was old but so finely woven that the water did not leak through it.

The photo we have of Inigo was published in the *San Francisco Chronicle* in 1903, submitted by California pioneer Edward A.T. Gallagher, who called Inigo the "last leaf on the tree" of Mission Santa Clara.

In new details I've uncovered since my book was published, I've learned more about the photographer, William Shew, who created Inigo's portrait. He was well known in San Francisco after his arrival in 1851, as a former student of Samuel F.B. Morse. He came to California at the suggestion of John Wesley Jones to take pictures for an exhibit Jones was planning with the unwieldy name "The Great Pantoscope of California, the Rocky Mountains, Salt Lake City, Nebraska, and Kansas." Shew set up a mobile studio in a wagon he located in several places in downtown San Francisco in the 1850s.

This information might explain how and why Inigo's photographic portrait was created. It is possible he was persuaded to sit for it as a representative of his people. His neighbor Alfred Doten later told a reporter he recalled riding with Inigo to Mountain View one day. "The old fellow says when he was a little boy, his tribe was numerous about here, but all have died and he is the only one left." The conversation was cited by Laurence H. Shoup in a 1995 report to Santa Clara County. Shoup also wrote that Inigo is believed to have been the "old chief" who consulted with Father Gregory Mengarini at Santa Clara College, now Santa Clara University, for a 1855 article, "The Indian Language of the Santa Clara Valley." If true, this shows Inigo was active in helping historians gather information about his people.

William Shew, the photographer, had a mobile studio. This would have made it possible for Shew to bring his equipment to the Santa Clara Valley, saving Inigo the difficult trip to San Francisco—difficult especially for a man his age with a working ranch. Until the rail came through to Mountain View, the journey to San Francisco could take three days.

However this photograph came about, we are fortunate to have it. Study it and you will see it tells us a great deal about this man. He is wearing a homespun suit that is neat and well cared for. His exposed right hand is the hand of a working man. In his left is a staff—a symbol of his status. His hair and beard are turning white. One of the most striking things about him is that he looks so tired. Lope Inigo worked hard, and his life was

Lope Inigo in 1856 when he was seventy-five years old. The photograph is by William Shew of San Francisco. *Courtesy History San José.*

hard. Within two years, he would lose his second wife, Eustaquia, and their newborn child to childbirth.

He lived long enough to see the telegraph completed between the eastern United States and San Francisco in 1861 and to see the railroad line open between San Francisco and San Jose—with a stop in Mountain View. A month after the rail stop opened, Inigo fell ill. He sent for a priest and asked to be buried on his ranch near a cross he had planted. He was eighty-three years old when he died and was buried near the smaller of two Ohlone mounds on his property.

Thanks in part to his photograph, he has not been forgotten. He is remembered on a marker that features the picture, on the platform of the NASA/Bayshore station on the VTA light rail line near the Ellis Gate at Moffett Field. He is the only California Indigenous man known to be so featured.

The exact location of Inigo's final resting place has been lost. Somewhere out there on the edge of the Bay amid Silicon Valley's sprawl and the bones of his ancestors, Lope Inigo has finally found his rest.

JUANA AND HER MYSTERY PHOTO

Juana Briones was born near California's Mission Santa Cruz in 1802, the child of Spanish, Mexican, Indian and African ancestors. In 1776, her parents were among the first group of settlers from what was then New Spain to immigrate to California—her mother as a three-year-old child. Juana was born in California, and her life, like Inigo's, contains a photograph with a mystery.

During her lifetime, she was beloved for her kindness and care in nursing the sick and for her acumen in business, which gained her land and wealth. The evidence suggests she did not know how to read or write—unheard of for a woman in business today but not unusual in the Spanish and Mexican cultures of that time. Juana did not let this hold her back. Throughout her life, she hired lawyers and scribes when she needed paperwork done. We have many of her documents on the record in California history.

With her husband, the soldier Apolinario Miranda, Juana lived for many years in the tiny village that became San Francisco. In the years between 1843 and 1850, she purchased Rancho La Purísima Concepción in the Santa Clara Valley from Ohlone Indians José Gorgonio and José Ramon, who, like Inigo, had received their ranch as a land grant from the Mexican government. The two men and their families stayed on to help Juana manage the property, which, at 4,438.94 acres, was considerably larger than the ranch of Lope Inigo.

Rancho La Purísima Concepción included most of the land that became Los Altos Hills and some of the land that became Los Altos, Stanford University and Palo Alto. It gave Juana room to expand her dairy and cattle business, increasingly cramped on the sandy hills near the Presidio. But we do not believe this is the only reason she bought it. Beginning in 1840, when Juana was pregnant with her last child, she reported her husband a dozen times to the Presidio magistrate—the *alcalde*—for assaults so severe that Apolinario was several times put in jail. In one incident, he hit Juana with the flat side of a broadsword, knocked her down and opened a gash on the back of her head. An Indigenous man ran for help while another stood by to protect her.

Juana may have decided to move from San Francisco for her own safety.

In H.H. Bancroft's *California Pioneer Register and Index*, he adds next to her husband's entry: "In [18]'43 in trouble with his wife." It was in 1843 that Juana made the long journey from the Presidio to Mission Santa Clara seeking a legal separation from her husband—the best she could hope for in a Catholic society that did not allow divorce. It was not for her own sake, but for the sake of her children, she told the padre: "[B]ecause from him they learn nothing but swearing and blasphemy and ugly, lewd, and dissolute behavior." When church authorities read her testimony, they took steps to protect her, and she was allowed to record the title to Rancho La Purísima Concepción in her own name—rare for a married woman at that time.

Juana Briones left her mark on Los Altos Hills in ways she could not have imagined. Here's a modern street sign featuring her family name. *Photo by Robin Chapman.*

There is no record that the separation was granted, but afterward, she was often referred to as the "widow Briones." Apolinario Miranda made it official when, in 1847, he died at the age of fifty-four. Since she was still his legal wife, Juana inherited their joint property, and she hired lawyers to prove up her claims in the new American courts after 1850. She was successful in all of them, taking one case—and winning it—up to the Supreme Court of the United States.

Facing so many challenges, Juana Briones found time to be compassionate. During this same period, she adopted an orphaned Indigenous girl, giving her a home and the Briones name.

Juana prospered on her ranch, enjoying many happy days there. Her sister Guadalupe married into the Miramontes clan of Half Moon Bay and came over the hills in summer for an annual fiesta, bringing along her large and musical family, which, according to historian Mildred Brooke Hoover, "formed a whole brass band and added much to the gaiety of the occasion."

Like Lope Inigo, Juana Briones lived a long life. She left her ranch to move down to Mayfield in 1884, only in the last years of her life. Mayfield was an early Palo Alto townsite that developed along El Camino Real near what is now California Avenue. Juana, born into a world of adobe houses and dirt floors, lived there in a wood frame home, down the street from the train station and the telegraph office and around the corner from an innovative kindergarten founded by her neighbor, Mrs. Leland Stanford.

Juana Briones y Tapia de Miranda died in Mayfield in 1889. She was eighty-seven years old and left a fortune in land to her large and extended family.

For many years, there were no known images of her. Then, in 2007, descendants of the Garcia family, into which Juana's brother had married,

Left: The mystery photo, believed to be Juana Briones, was donated by her descendants in 2007 to a Bay Area museum. *Courtesy Point Reyes National Seashore Archive.*

Right: We do have an authenticated photo of Juana's brother Gregorio Briones, one of the founders of the city of Bolinas. His features are similar to those of the woman in the photo believed to be Juana Briones—note especially his mouth. *Courtesy Bolinas Museum History Archives, Thomas Barfield Collection, 1983.2.2.*

donated a nineteenth-century studio photographic portrait of a woman to a Marin museum, saying it had been passed down for seven generations as a photograph of their ancestor Juana Briones.

"There is debate as to whether it is her, both in her looks and in the medium of the portrait, which is a platinum print," said Carola DeRooy, who in 2017 was the archivist and collections manager at the Point Reyes National Seashore Museum, which owns the photograph. "Platinum prints only came into vogue in the early 1890s, and that was after her death," she said.

An expert consulted by the museum, however, said the photograph could be a reprint of an earlier original, which would explain the medium of the print and the 1850s clothing on the woman. DeRooy agreed the photo does bear a resemblance to known photos of Juana's other family members.

Recently, I called the curator of Marin Art and History at the Bolinas Museum, Elia Haworth, about the Juana photograph. I had seen an authenticated photograph of Juana's brother Gregorio, one of the founders of the city of Bolinas, and noticed how similar his mouth was to the mouth of the woman in the photograph, believed to be Juana. "It is so definitely the Briones mouth," Haworth agreed when I spoke with her. So much so, she admitted she had made a montage of photographs of Briones relatives showing all of them with the straight-in-a-line-across-the-face kind of mouth, so evident in the photo believed to be of Juana. "Family stories aren't always accurate," said Haworth. "But family attributes can tell us a lot."

The mention of the 1850s clothing by the museum expert is intriguing. It suggests a possible date for the original photo of Juana—if it is Juana—that is very close in time to the Lope Inigo portrait of 1856. Juana would have been in her early fifties then, and the portrait does appear to be of a woman about that age. Like Inigo, Juana was, by the 1850s, a survivor of California's early pioneer days. It is possible that she, too, may have had her photograph taken for that exhibit about the West developed by William Shew. At this point, we can only speculate. But each piece of evidence we find makes historians more comfortable in identifying the photograph as Juana Briones.

Juana Briones often seems to have been a woman out of her time. She checked none of the boxes we expect of a well-known woman of history. She didn't lead an army, a country, a revolution or a criminal enterprise. Juana Briones was unique and self-created. Some of the smartest people on the planet now live on her land. She had it first. Tough in business and successful, she never forgot to be compassionate. Her story is unlikely, which is why it is so intriguing. In debt to no one for the woman she became, she was entirely self-invented.

I like to think we see this strength in her photograph. One day, perhaps, we will know for sure.

THOMAS FOON CHEW AND NEW INFORMATION

Thomas Foon Chew was very well known in California during his lifetime. We know this because not only was his death covered by newspapers in both San Jose and San Francisco, but also because his family tradition says he had two funerals—one in each of those cities. He was a multimillionaire in the canning business when he died in San Jose in 1931. But his story was no longer widely known when I found a few lines about his life in an out-of-print book in 2012. I began to investigate, and in 2018, I included a chapter about him in *Historic Bay Area Visionaries*, the first lengthy work on Thomas Foon (as he liked to be called) in nearly half a century. In 2019, he was back in the news as preservationists worked to save the remains of his canneries in Alviso and Palo Alto.

I've continued to learn about him since I first uncovered his story.

He came to San Francisco from China as an eight-year-old, reportedly from the Loong Kai District of Guangdong Province, in about 1897. A man called Sai Yen Chew, who said he was the boy's father, brought the young man with a woman he said was the boy's mother. How this immigration was possible in the era of the Chinese Exclusion Acts of 1882 is one of the mysteries—though Thomas Foon's granddaughter Gloria Hom of Palo Alto told me that her grandmother often said, "People who had the money could always go back and forth."

The couple had no other children, also unusual in Chinese families of that era. It is possible Sai Yen Chew brought a widowed sister to America with her son, or she may have been a sister-in-law. This is something we may never know, but it was not unheard of then.

After my book came out, the Los Altos History Museum shared my research as part of an exhibition called "Silicon Valley Eats," an appropriate link, since Foon was known during his lifetime as the "Asparagus King" for perfecting the commercial canning of green asparagus. His last surviving son, Timothy Chew, a Berkeley grad born in 1924, was abroad during my initial research, and I didn't get the chance to interview him. But in 2019, he returned, toured the Los Altos exhibit and, with the help of Gloria Hom—Foon's granddaughter and Timothy's niece—we finally met.

Timothy was just a small boy when his father died. But he recalled his father's asthma, for which the family sought the clear air of Los Gatos, becoming the first Chinese family to buy a home there. Timothy also remembered that the asthma hadn't stopped his father from chain-smoking cigars. I asked Timothy how he thought his family had managed to immigrate to America during the days of the Chinese Exclusion Acts. Timothy said his mother told him the family came on a work visa set aside for Chinese merchants, an exception to the laws of that time. Timothy is a good source: for many years, he served as an agent for the CIA. When I spoke with him, he said it was okay to report this, since he was in his nineties and long retired.

We got together with Timothy and his wife, Sally, at the Chew home in San Francisco. A few months later, before the pandemic closed so many borders, they departed for their annual trip to Australia, where they also have family. On the journey, Timothy Chew's cancer, which had been in remission, returned, and as Sally wrote to me later, "he passed very gently in Perth, on February 25, 2020." He was ninety-five years old—the last direct link to his father.

Timothy Chew, holding a toy horse, poses with an unknown friend on an ocean liner journey to Hong Kong. He was just six years old when his father died in 1931. *Courtesy Sally Chew.*

More new information came to me from Fred Wool, the last president of the Muirson Label Company of San Jose. Wool read about my research on Foon and contacted me to say he had a stash of labels he wanted to dispose of, which were designed and printed for Thomas Foon's Bay Side Cannery.

Gloria Hom and I drove to San Jose to meet Wool at his office and to look at his files. As we reviewed the collection, we learned Bay Side canned under at least seven different brand names—something you often see today but that we were not aware Thomas Foon did back in the early twentieth century. Some of his brand names in addition to Bay Side included Bohemian, Cal Taste, Gondolier, Calico and Snow Peak. This was all new information to Thomas Foon Chew's family and to me.

Two of the many brands produced by Thomas Foon Chew's Bay Side Canning Company (sometimes also spelled Bayside and BaySide). Thomas Foon, as he liked to be called, was known as the "Asparagus King" for being the first to successfully preserve delicate green asparagus stalks in a can. *Author's collection.*

In 1931, when Foon contracted pneumonia, he was admitted to O'Connor Sanitarium, now O'Connor Hospital. Antibiotics as a common treatment for pneumonia were not available until the 1940s, and Foon did not survive. His death made news on February 25, 1931, on page 3 of the *San Jose Mercury Herald* under the headline "Funeral Rites for Thos. Chew to Be Delayed," a delay caused by the fact that he died during the celebration of the Chinese New Year.

In *Historic Bay Area Visionaries*, I feature a photograph of his funeral, loaned to me by his granddaughter, who was not sure where the photo was taken but thought it was taken at his memorial in San Jose. After my book's publication, a reader asked me where in San Jose this took place, and I didn't know, so I

Thomas Foon Chew's funeral was delayed from February 1931 until May due to the celebration of the Chinese New Year. Shown here, it was finally held along Grant Avenue in San Francisco. *Courtesy Gloria Hom.*

consulted Michael Lara, a reference librarian at the Dr. Martin Luther King Jr. Library. We both examined the photograph with magnifying glasses, and Lara was able to research the businesses identified on the awnings shown in the photo. As it turns out, the photograph was not taken in San Jose. It is of his funeral procession along one of the most famous routes in America: Grant Avenue, San Francisco, California, USA (as it says in the Rodgers and Hammerstein song), the heart of the West's largest Chinatown. Twenty-five thousand people turned out to honor Thomas Foon Chew that day in 1931.

It was a tribute to a man who broke many barriers in California and whose fascinating life story is at last being rediscovered.

THE WOMAN HE LOVED

Earlier in my research, I focused on one key aspect of the story of writer Robert Louis Stevenson and his visit to California in 1879. I was intrigued by the idea that while he was here, Stevenson noticed the deterioration of the Carmel Mission and wrote about it. Though his visit to the Monterey area was brief, that article had a great impact, and not long afterward, the Carmel Mission got a new roof and a preservation movement was born in California.

In the years since, I've thought a lot more about California's impact on Robert Louis Stevenson. This wild state had to be an enormous contrast to the world he knew in Scotland and Europe. It is possible that these very differences captured his imagination, for after his visit, his creative work soared.

When he came to California, Stevenson was just twenty-eight years old and not yet famous as a writer. On August 30, 1879, he arrived in San Francisco after a long journey first by steamship from Glasgow to New York and then across America on the first transcontinental railroad. He had been traveling for nearly a month.

"The day was breaking as we crossed the ferry," he wrote. "[T]he fog was rising over the citied hills of San Francisco; the bay was perfect—not a ripple, scarce a stain, upon its blue expanse; everything was waiting, breathless for the sun."

Stevenson had published articles in prestigious journals in England and had written two travel books—*An Inland Voyage* and *Travels with a Donkey*. These gained him some attention but not much fame or fortune.

He was in California on a nonliterary trek. Three years before, in France, he had met and fallen in love with a California woman named Fanny Osbourne. Now, he had traveled six thousand miles to persuade her to marry him, even though she was, rather inconveniently, married to someone else.

Fanny lived in Oakland with her husband, their son Lloyd and daughter, Belle, and had recently decamped to Monterey to put some distance between herself and her chronically unfaithful spouse. Sam Osbourne was a Civil War veteran, a cheerful rogue and one of the founders of the Bohemian Club.

Stevenson was so anxious to see Fanny, he did not even pause in what was, even then, the famous City by the Bay. In the years since I first wrote about him, I have been able to learn more about how RLS traveled in the Golden State: California may have had little in common with the world he left behind, but it did have railroads.

At the ferry landing, he may have walked to the rail station, since he loved walking. But since he was in a new city and exhausted from a long journey, he likely caught a horse car on Market Street—like a trolley but pulled by a horse—which would have taken him from the ferry landing to the depot of the Southern Pacific (SP) Railroad at Fourth and Townsend.

He bought a ticket to Salinas on the SP—since Salinas was as close as that line came to Monterey. In San Francisco that morning, he boarded an SP train pulled by a steam locomotive, which chugged south from San Francisco into the Santa Clara Valley. We can thus say with certainty that RLS spent time in the Santa Clara Valley—though most of that time was spent traveling through it.

As the train rolled along, Stevenson saw the acres of orchards and the rural fields filled with cattle. It was August, and much of the fruit from the Valley of Heart's Delight had gone to market.

A photograph of Robert Louis Stevenson at the age of thirty-seven wearing one of his iconic blue velvet jackets. It is believed this photo was taken by Fanny Osbourne's daughter, Belle. *Courtesy Monterey Historic State Park.*

The long, low whistle of a train still has the power to evoke the ache of longing and the mystery of travel. On that day in 1879, the train's whistle at the valley's crossings may have meant all that and more to Stevenson. He still had no idea what would happen when he finally saw Fanny Osbourne after their years apart.

According to the timetables of 1879, he arrived in Salinas about 1:30 p.m. and had to change trains and stations. He had to get himself and his luggage across town to the station of the new Monterey & Salinas Valley Railroad, which would take him to the Monterey wharf.

The only son of a wealthy engineer, Stevenson suffered from lung disease—what kind is still debated among scholars. Whatever it was, it caused him repeated hemorrhages and fevers throughout his life. At five feet, ten inches tall, he weighed only 118 pounds when he left Edinburgh, and he wrote friends to say he had lost about ten pounds on his journey. He had also acquired a rash on his face and hands, so he wasn't looking his best when he finally arrived in Monterey.

The village where he stepped off the train had once been the capital of Mexican California but was now a settlement of only about 350 people, though it had most recently been gaining a reputation as an artists' colony. In a town so small, in a time of Victorian proprieties, Stevenson may not have felt it seemly for a bachelor to call on a married woman with his luggage in hand. He stopped at the Bohemian Saloon near the wharf, took time to brace himself with a brandy and to chat with the locals and decided to leave his luggage to be called for later. He learned Fanny and her family—everybody except her husband—were living nearby in rented rooms at the Bonifacio adobe.

Fanny's son Lloyd remembered what happened next. "I remember his walking into the room," he wrote, "and the outcry of delight that greeted him." There were tears as Stevenson and Fanny Osbourne embraced. "Now he looked ill," wrote Lloyd, "even to my childish gaze.…His clothes no longer picturesque but merely shabby, hung loosely on his shrunken body."

Fanny Osbourne was eleven years older than Stevenson, and with a husband and family to consider, she did not immediately accept his proposal of marriage. Then, within just a few weeks, Fanny's husband came to visit. To get out of the way—or perhaps to gain perspective—Stevenson rented a horse and cart and went exploring in the direction of the Carmel Valley, saying he was looking for better air beyond the fogs of Monterey.

He was found a few days later unconscious under a tree by two ranchers who nursed him back to health. While he recovered in their care, he began writing again—an early draft of the story of his journey to America, later published as *The Amateur Emigrant* and *Across the Plains.*

Even when he returned to Monterey, he was still pretty sick. His new friend, restaurateur Jules Simoneau, found him one day on the floor of his boardinghouse, ill with a fever, and had to call in a local physician, Dr. J.P. Heintz. After the doctor departed, it was an old Indian woman named Jacinta who nursed Stevenson. She is the one who found an herb that cured his rash, which, says author Roy Nickerson, "the man of medicine…had failed to do."

Perhaps it was his fragile health and his disappearance into the Carmel hills—or maybe it was the disappearance of that nasty rash—but Fanny relented. On October 21, 1879—about six weeks after Stevenson arrived in Monterey—the woman he loved returned to her cottage in Oakland and filed for divorce.

After RLS married Fanny Osbourne in San Francisco, he arranged to have this picture taken of her to send to his parents in Scotland. *Courtesy Robert Louis Stevenson Club of Edinburgh.*

CHRISTMAS IN CALIFORNIA

Christmas 1879 should have been a happy one for Robert Louis Stevenson. He had met Fanny in France in 1876 and had become besotted with this American creature who rolled her own cigarettes and liked to slip off her shoes as they talked, perching her tiny feet on the nearest chair. She was like no woman he had ever met.

Stevenson had been devastated when she returned to her husband in California. He had traveled six thousand miles to win her and was very close to doing so. He had secured her promise to divorce her husband and marry him.

Now he just had to wait.

In December 1879, the divorce came through. When Stevenson got the news in Monterey, he headed to San Francisco to be near her. He now retraced the route he had traveled in August. He caught the Monterey & Salinas Valley Railroad back to Salinas and got back across town to catch the next SP train to San Francisco. As the train wound its way from Salinas to Gilroy and then north through the Santa Clara Valley, he could see the orchards in their winter rest.

In San Francisco, he found a tiny apartment on Bush Street and made friends with his landlord and with the waiters at nearby restaurants. His future with Fanny looked bright, and he hoped soon to reconcile with his family in Scotland. He was an only child, and his parents were stunned by his adventure. Still, with a wedding now in his future, his Christmas in San Francisco promised to be a happy one.

But it was not to be.

Fanny—afraid of appearances, perhaps, or troubled by the decisions ahead—spent Christmas with her family, including her husband, Sam. Robert Louis Stevenson spent Christmas alone. As he wrote to a friend on December 26, 1879: "For four days I have spoken to no one but my landlady or landlord, or to restaurant waiters. This is not a gay way to pass Christmas, is it?"

But none of us can know what lies ahead. One bad day—or one bad Christmas—does not necessarily forecast the future.

On that Christmas, Stevenson was on the brink of both happiness and success. A few months later, after he fell ill again, Fanny took it upon herself to nurse him back to health. This time, his condition was so bad he couldn't even hold a pen for six weeks. Yet the couple set a date for their wedding, and he gradually recovered.

Above: The stories Stevenson wrote after he left San Francisco gained world renown. This vintage postcard promotes the 1934 MGM movie *Treasure Island* featuring Wallace Beery as Long John Silver and Jackie Cooper as Jim Hawkins. Cooper later said he liked making the movie but hated wearing that wig. *Author's collection.*

Opposite: Stevenson's life, like his stories, was filled with adventure. This is Stevenson, *far right*, aboard the schooner *Casco* in the South Pacific, 1888. *Courtesy Monterey Historic State Park.*

On May 19, 1880, nine months after Stevenson arrived in California, he found a willing Presbyterian minister, Dr. William Scott, and the couple married at the Scott home at 521 Post Street, San Francisco, with Mrs. Scott serving as one of the witnesses. The couple's friend Dora Williams served as the other. Then Fanny, RLS and Dora went to the Viennese Bakery for a wedding dinner. Fanny later wrote that the couple honeymooned for the first two days at San Francisco's Palace Hotel. Later, they went on a longer journey with Fanny's son Lloyd at the remains of a silver mine in the Napa Valley, a sojourn featured in Stevenson's book *The Silverado Squatters*.

With Fanny at his side, Stevenson returned to Scotland—to the great relief of his parents, who wired the couple the money for a first-class trip home. The next seven years were among the richest of his creative life and included the publication of many of the books we still read today: *Treasure Island, Kidnapped, A Child's Garden of Verses, Strange Case of Dr. Jekyll and Mr. Hyde* and *New Arabian Nights*. The work brought him wealth and international acclaim and a reputation that continues into the present century.

Writer Roy Nickerson thinks it was California that changed his work. In *Robert Louis Stevenson in California*, he writes, "Without California, and therefore without Fanny, RLS may have remained an unsung travel writer. In California, he came upon the foreign scenes and the foreign people, all of which jolted him from his rather leisurely approach to life, providing him with fresh material and a mother lode of personalities to populate his stories." The couple later traveled the South Seas together—an experience that also influenced his work—and settled in Samoa, where Stevenson died in 1894.

But what of Fanny's impact? Some say Fanny was a great muse. Some say she was a loving nurse. Some say she loved money, and Stevenson worked hard to pay the bills. Who knows what sparks a writer's imagination?

Chapter 4

LIVING HISTORY

*Little remained of California's eighth mission
but scattered stands of blackened adobe.
—Gerald McKevitt*

I n the Santa Clara Valley, there are many modern buildings but very few that go back more than a century. One of the oldest still in use should be Mission Santa Clara de Asís. But is it?

MISSION SANTA CLARA

The world was shocked to see the fire that came close to burning down the cathedral of Notre-Dame de Paris in 2019. That remarkable building is not only an icon we associate with Paris, but it has also been part of French life for nearly nine hundred years.

Santa Clara County also has an important connection to an ancient church. The county is named after Mission Santa Clara de Asís, established in the valley by Spanish-speaking immigrants in 1777. But as you may learn when you visit there, the present building known as Mission Santa Clara does not go back that far. Like Notre-Dame de Paris, it, too, had to be rebuilt after a devastating fire.

During its years as a colonial outpost, Mission Santa Clara was moved three times and rebuilt five. Rivers and creeks surprised the Spanish padres by looking dry and peaceful in the summer and then overflowing their banks in winter. Floods caused the first few moves. Earthquakes and fires also played their parts. The mission was moved to its present site at 500 El Camino Real in what is now the city of Santa Clara—also named after the church—in the nineteenth century. Its last Franciscan edifice was dedicated there in 1825, just about the time Mexico gained its independence from Spain.

Its early role as a mission to California's Indigenous people makes it controversial today. But it was a mission church for just seventy-four years. The majority of its life since—nearly two centuries—Santa Clara de Asís has been a parish church and a college chapel.

The condition of the property was "wretched," according to the local bishop, when he turned it over to the Jesuits for a school in 1851, shortly after California achieved statehood. During the transitions from Spanish to Mexican to American rule, the mission and its land were neglected and plundered. The church was used as a stable and then as a hotel for pioneers. One of its buildings—the former fourth mission church—had become a fandango parlor operated by the mistress of its last Franciscan priest. The Jesuits had to buy it back from her. The fruit of its neglected orchards was appropriated by entrepreneurs during the Gold Rush and sold in San Francisco.

The Jesuits cleaned up the mess and opened Santa Clara College in 1851, filling an important need at a time when there were almost no schools in California. By 1926, this fifth iteration of the mission church was 101 years old and at the center of a small but successful educational institution.

On October 24, 1926, just as the priest finished his early morning Matins, about 7:00 a.m., fire broke out in the north bell tower of the old building and quickly burned out of control, apparently ignited by faulty wiring. Students and faculty were able to save many artifacts—statues, paintings and liturgical vessels from the Spanish era—but much was lost. Says college historian Gerald McKevitt, "Augustin Dávila's ceiling paintings and the brightly colored reredos [ornamental screens] that had survived a sea voyage from Mexico in 1802 were lost forever, as were many documents and relics housed in the office of the pastor of the church." By the end of the day, the building was, he wrote, a "heap of ruins and ashes."

Thus, the present church is Mission Santa Clara's sixth iteration, built in twentieth-century concrete and painted in the muted colors of the Arts and Crafts style, which make it lovely but not an exact replica of the old mission. Descriptions tell us earlier versions featured pigments of crimson and yellow, with the exterior covered in bright murals. There were three mission bells in

Mission Santa Clara burning, October 24, 1926. In the chaos of the fire, it is remarkable this photo was taken that day. *Courtesy Department of Archives & Special Collections, Santa Clara University.*

use at the time of the blaze, two of which had been donated by Charles IV of Spain, and both of those were damaged beyond repair. The third, which had been cast in Mexico in 1798, survived and was raised onto a scaffold the evening of the fire to toll *De Profundis*, a prayer for the dead. Wrote the university's historian, "The somber tones rang across the mission gardens as they had for more than a hundred years."

You can still tour Mission Santa Clara, enjoy its beauty and see history nearby. Next to the present church is a single adobe wall—the last piece of the old building that was not consumed in the 1926 fire.

The new Mission Santa Clara de Asís was completed in 1929. That means this sixth version of the old mission is now heading toward its century mark—gaining some historic gravitas of its own.

Just eight more centuries, and it will be right up there—age wise—with Notre-Dame de Paris.

MISSION BELL MARKERS

Longtime Saratoga resident John Kolstad has spent much of the twenty-first century working to preserve and restore the well-known Mission Bell Markers that have graced California's El Camino Real and other historic places of interest for the better part of the last century.

The original markers were designed by Mrs. A.S.C. Forbes in the early twentieth century to identify the seven-hundred-mile route traveled by the first Spanish-speaking immigrants to California. The poles recall the shape of the shepherds' crooks used as walking sticks by some of the travelers. Each of these poles holds an eighty-five-pound cast-iron bell—evocative of the early California adobes.

The original ones also held directional signs and mileage to the next city. That was because in the early days of the automobile, California had no road signs. Installed in 1906 and paid for by chapters of the Federated Women's Clubs of California, these early markers became California's first highway markers. Mrs. Forbes, director of the Historical Society of Southern California and a Women's Club member, had to start her own company, buy her own foundry and forge her own bells in order to produce the signs. In the course of this, she became the only woman bell maker in the United States.

A Mission Bell Marker installed by the State of California along the El Camino Real in Mountain View. *Photo by Robin Chapman.*

Simple in design and execution, many of the markers and their original bells were lost to theft and new highway construction by the time the state took on their care in 1959. In the year 2000, John Kolstad began a quest to find just one of the old bells for his garden. He tracked down what remained of Mrs. Forbes's California Bell Company to its third owner, octogenarian Joe Rice, in La Crescenta, California.

"He had old bells, company files and bell molds floor-to-ceiling in his garage," Kolstad says. "I made him an offer and bought what remained of the company."

Keith Robinson was then the principal landscape architect for Caltrans and worked with Kolstad to restore the markers. With the help of federal grants, Kolstad helped Robinson and Caltrans produce 585 new Mission Bell Markers up and down the old El Camino—from Sonoma to San Diego—many installed just in time for the markers' 2006 centennial. Cities like Gilroy ordered extras to identify their landmarks.

Californians seem to feel strongly about these markers, as the bells are still today frequently stolen off their poles. Yet their popularity is not universal. The City of Santa Cruz had three of the markers on city land, and in recent years, the council there voted to remove them at the urging of the Amah Mutsun tribal band, which found the bells a reminder of the mission era and offensive. Two were taken down. The third one was scheduled to be removed in a ceremony in August 2021. But the night before the event, the bell was stolen.

In 2022, the City of Gilroy added a new Mission Bell Marker to its downtown.

As you drive the old routes traveled in the eighteenth century by the first Spanish-speaking immigrants to California, see if you can spot these markers along the roadways. Thanks to one Saratoga man, these signs still stand as reminders of the turbulent California story along our green and golden landscape.

Mrs. Winchester's Other House

A movie about the life of Sarah Winchester brought the actress Helen Mirren to San Jose briefly in 2017 to shoot a few scenes at the Winchester Mystery House. Mirren wasn't in the region long, since much of the filming for *Winchester* was done in Australia. That's because Winchester's original home, once surrounded by a large ranch and orchards, is now hemmed in by Interstate 280, a mobile home park, a mall, several big movie theaters and the eponymous Winchester Boulevard. The film about the historic home and its owner is not a memorable one. But the ghostly—if fanciful—story about its circumstances is apparently so interesting to people that it did make quite a lot of money.

There are, nevertheless, many more true tales to discover in the life of Sarah Winchester. There is even another house.

Sarah Winchester, heir to the Winchester Repeating Arms fortune, moved to California in 1886 after the death of her husband. There are myriad tales about her, many of them debunked by De Anza College professor Mary Jo

Ignoffo in her book *Captive of the Labyrinth*, published by the University of Missouri Press in 2010.

For starters, she was not the elderly recluse of legend. She was just forty-six when she moved to California and began remodeling the house on the estate she purchased near San Jose. And though she did live quietly in the quirky, always-under-construction mansion, she also bought and lived in quite a few other properties south of San Francisco. She had a houseboat in Burlingame, several estates in Atherton, more homes in Palo Alto and a lovely ranch in what is today Los Altos.

Winchester bought the Los Altos property—before there was a city called Los Altos—on 140 acres in 1888 for her sister and brother-in-law, Isabelle and Louis Merriman, who raised carriage horses and grew wholesale flowers there.

The original house dated back to the 1860s, with evidence of a structure there as early as 1840. The property was once a piece of the 4,440-acre Rancho San Antonio, granted to Juan Prado Mesa in 1839. Mesa, a soldier, died in 1845, badly in debt. His executor sold the land for seven cents an acre. People—especially realtors—gnash their teeth today in California when they hear numbers like that.

Winchester and her sister remodeled the existing home and expanded it from four rooms to more than a dozen. They added a Gothic window, which author Ignoffo notes "looks remarkably similar to one that had been on the house that Sarah was remodeling for herself." Another window is believed to have come from a San Jose church. The sisters added oblique angles, fish-scale shingles and intentionally mismatched windows and doors—hallmarks of stylish homes in the nineteenth century.

They called the home El Sueño, which the sisters translated as "The Daydream."

Between 1904 and 1905, Winchester learned that the Southern Pacific Railroad planned to bisect her ranch with a new track, roughly along the route of today's Foothill Expressway. Her lawyer informed her the company would pay her a small settlement based on the law of eminent domain. She believed this would devalue her property, since it would make it difficult for the horses on the ranch to get from their pasture near the site of today's downtown Los Altos to their watering hole at Adobe Creek—approximately where Shoup Park stands today.

While Winchester fought the plan, stories circulated that she and her sister went out at night and pulled up the railroad company's surveying stakes. Sarah Winchester was in her sixties by then, suffered from arthritis and was

The Winchester-Merriman House in Los Altos is a private residence and the community's oldest home. It retains many of the Carpenter Gothic flourishes installed by Sarah Winchester. *Photo by Robin Chapman.*

not a regular resident of El Sueño, so historians discount her role in any such activities. The railroad did, however, file a restraining order against the Merrimans and that "indicates the real culprits," according to Ignoffo.

After the 1906 earthquake devastated San Francisco and the region, Winchester gave in. But she won a major point. She insisted that because the railroad was damaging her property, the company should buy the entire ranch. Southern Pacific agreed and used the needed right-of-way for its new railroad and used more along that same corridor for its extension of the Peninsular Railway, the electric interurban line it was extending to Palo Alto. Then the SP flipped the rest of the property to executive Paul Shoup, who, with developer Walter Clark, subdivided the Winchester estate into building sites and a downtown, all now conveniently located along the SP Railroad and an electric commuter line.

Winchester's sister and brother-in-law were not good in business, and their debts and bankruptcies frustrated Sarah. Selling the place to the Southern Pacific and moving her sister into another property she owned in Palo Alto was a relief to her, though she hated being pushed around.

Authentic histories of Sarah Winchester's life debunk many of the myths about her. Yet one has to wonder who was responsible for giving the Winchester-Merriman House its City Historic Landmark plaque with that particular number. *Photo by Robin Chapman.*

That it all worked out was no consolation to Sarah Winchester, who wrote in a letter that it was just "one more distressing episode added to the list of harrowing experiences which I have met with since coming to California." Of course, by then she had also survived the 1906 earthquake.

Her large estate in San Jose, now called the Winchester Mystery House, suffered a lot of damage in the quake. Balconies fell down, and parts of the roof collapsed. She had it swept up and did not repair much of it. That resulted in at least some of the oddities that today entrance the tourists.

What happened to the other home, El Sueño?

Although it was large enough that it once served as a local school, the house was lovingly restored to a single-family residence in the twentieth century and is now the oldest occupied home in Los Altos. It sits on three-quarters of an acre under an enormous oak on Edgewood Lane. With the Coast Range as a backdrop, surrounded by wildflowers blooming in the sunshine, there appears to be not a single thing ghostly about the place. If you were looking for spirits there, they could be spotted—just briefly—when the house was on the market in 2018 and the realtor staged the sitting room to include a bar.

Yet Sarah Winchester did walk the halls here, so I would be wrong not to point out one curiosity. On the gatepost is the home's landmark plaque with its landmark number. I looked at it many times before I noticed that the house is City of Los Altos Historic Landmark No. 13.

WELCOME TO CALIFORNIA AT THE HOOVER PAVILION

You have probably driven past the Hoover Pavilion on El Camino Real at Quarry Road near Stanford Shopping Center many times. But you may not know its significance.

It was the region's first multistory structure or skyscraper, as the six-story structure was called back then, according to writer and historian Mary Feuer. Perhaps even more important, it was once Palo Alto's only hospital and as such the most popular place for Los Altos, Mountain View and Palo Alto babies to be born from the 1930s to the end of the 1950s. That's because it was the only place. El Camino Hospital in Mountain View did not open until 1961.

Don't get the Hoover Pavilion confused with Hoover Tower—that's another building entirely and is much taller and much deeper into the Stanford campus, and it wasn't built until 1941.

Palo Alto Hospital was first established in the 1890s. In 1931, the city opened its newest and last facility—in what is now called the Hoover Pavilion—at 285 Quarry Road. It was paid for by Palo Alto taxpayers on land leased from Stanford. The building had a unique Art Deco style and was designed so each of its hospital beds in the upstairs wards was near a window. This was a very modern feature for a hospital built nearly a century ago. And it was a thoughtful feature in a valley as beautiful as this one.

A photo of the old Palo Alto Hospital, now the Hoover Pavilion, taken in 1932, shortly after it opened. Newspapers dubbed it the region's first skyscraper. *Courtesy Palo Alto Historical Association.*

Unfortunately, the facility had trouble keeping pace with the region's booming birth rate, especially after World War II. After several additions, which didn't enhance its look, Palo Alto taxpayers grew tired of supporting the cost. In 1959, Stanford's Medical School moved south from San Francisco, Stanford University built a new medical facility on its campus and Palo Alto got out of the hospital business for good.

Between 2010 and 2012, Stanford renovated the old building, preserving its unique architecture and repurposing its eighty-two thousand square feet for new clinics and a medical library. In today's Silicon Valley, where old buildings are often demolished, this gem really shines. The Hoover Pavilion is now eligible for inclusion in both the California and the National Registers of Historic Places.

During the building's grand reopening, volunteers handed out "I Was Born at Hoover" stickers and found they were a hit. Lots of locals, it seems, fostered fond feelings for the place where they first opened their eyes, met their parents and gazed out those upper-story windows for their very first glimpses of this valley and the foothills beyond.

FRANK LLOYD WRIGHT IN THE ORCHARD

Architect Frank Lloyd Wright paid a visit to the Santa Clara Valley in 1954, gave a lecture series at Stanford University, toured the new headquarters of *Sunset Magazine* on the Peninsula and, as if that were not enough to keep the octogenarian busy, helped city officials in Los Altos pick the site for the newly incorporated city's civic center. It is a little-known story today.

Buried in a local article I found during research on another project, former mayor George Estill Sr. and retired building inspector Joseph Salameda reminisced about how the J. Gilbert Smith orchard property was selected for the Los Altos Civic Center.

It happened, they said, with the help of Frank Lloyd Wright. This was an important detail not included in the headline or even the early paragraphs of a *Los Altos Town Crier* article of July 8, 1981, headlined "Oldtimers Recall Los Altos' Past." Editor and reporter Doris "Tuck" Shepherd seriously buried her lead. You had to read more than half the article to learn about Wright's visit to Los Altos. "We were fortunate enough to have him tour the sites under consideration and give his thoughts," Joseph Salameda told Shepherd deep into the piece. Salameda was the city's entire building department in 1954 and later became its historian.

When Frank Lloyd Wright visited Stanford in 1954, he stayed at this house on the Stanford campus, a home he had designed for his friends Paul and Jean Hanna. *Courtesy Palo Alto Historical Association.*

I visited the archives of the old *Palo Alto Times* at the City of Palo Alto Library and discovered Frank Lloyd Wright did pay a well-publicized visit to Stanford University in February 1954, fourteen months after Los Altos incorporated and just about the time the city was searching for a place to build its city hall. During his visit, he stayed with Dr. Paul Hanna and his wife, Jean, in a house Wright had designed for them in 1936 on the Stanford campus. By 1954, Wright's interests had grown beyond residential design, as the *Stanford Daily* noted: "He has extended his originality to commercial and industrial design and has also been concerned with community planning."

Flying in to the Bay Area on February 10, 1954, Wright was fêted at a Stanford dinner that night and then at a public lecture where Dean Ray Faulkner introduced him as "America's greatest living architect." According to the *Palo Alto Times*, "The audience jammed Memorial Hall and filled the Little Theatre for a broadcast of his talk." The next morning, Wright met with reporters, held a seminar, ate lunch with students and then, the newspaper reported, planned to leave the campus.

We know he did leave campus that day, since *Sunset Magazine* publisher Bill Lane later wrote it was February 11, 1954, that Wright toured the new

Cliff May–designed headquarters of Lane's "Magazine of Western Living." The new building—sold in 2014 and no longer the home of *Sunset*—was a Mission Revival structure surrounded by nine acres of landscaped gardens. Wright had been critical of Stanford's architecture, calling it a "confused mass of disassociated buildings in a bastard style of architecture," according to the *Palo Alto Times* of Thursday, February 11, 1954. In contrast, Wright told publisher Bill Lane, *"Sunset Magazine* is the best building I have seen all day!" No wonder Lane quoted this and used a photo of Wright visiting *Sunset*'s headquarters in his autobiography.

Wright was scheduled to depart the next day, so it seems likely it was just after his visit to Menlo Park that Wright came to Los Altos, just ten miles from the magazine's Willow Road address. Los Altos had several sites in mind for its city hall, including one near El Monte Avenue at what is now Foothill Expressway—then still the railroad tracks—as well as the J. Gilbert Smith property on San Antonio Road. "He decided the Smith place was the best for several reasons—the trees, the heritage of Smith's [orchard] and the fact that it was one of the earliest houses," Joseph Salameda told the *Los Altos Town Crier* in 1981. "There was also more space available than at the others. It was rather apparent this was the spot."

Los Altos resident George Estill Jr., a Stanford alum and son of the former mayor, told me before his death in 2021 that his father had met Wright in Chicago and the two men had kept in touch. Estill said his father hoped Wright would design the new Los Altos Civic Center. Unfortunately, the city treasury was so bare in those days, officials had to pay for their own postage, so it was not to be. And time was running out for Wright.

A 1954 photo of Frank Lloyd Wright by *New York World–Telegram and Sun* photographer Al Ravenna. *Author's collection.*

Although local papers reported he was eighty-four during his 1954 visit, he was actually just shy of his eighty-seventh birthday. Three years later, he did design the new Marin Civic Center, but he did not live to see it built. He died in 1959 at the age of ninety-one.

Yet Wright took time out to help a new community make a critical decision. With his vision, he saw a plot of land that would incorporate future and past in the organic style of architecture he promoted. It was a working orchard then with apricot trees, a hand-built home and a view of the Coast Range. Today, the space still encompasses the old home—now a history house—and the orchard along with the civic center. And the Los Altos Heritage Orchard is still a working orchard.

It is truly a space that can be celebrated for the day a white-haired genius joined young city leaders to dream big dreams one February afternoon.

ALL ELECTRIC TRANSPORT

At the Saratoga Historical Foundation Museum at 20450 Saratoga–Los Gatos Road, an interesting place in its own right, there is something unusual on the edge of the parking lot. It is a covered bench that looks like a trolley stop with a sign on it that reads "Peninsular Railway" and under that "Nippon Mura." It is indeed an old stop from the days of the Peninsular Railroad, an electric interurban line. A group of volunteers found the stop stashed in the garden of a recently deceased member. They scooped it up and lovingly restored it when they had some off-time during the Covid-19 pandemic. It featured the name Nippon Mura because there was a resort by that name between Saratoga and Los Gatos owned by a family who had spent many years in Japan. The stop shows how the Peninsular created this tiny depot to serve visitors to the Santa Clara Valley.

The San Jose and Los Gatos Interurban Railroad under construction about 1902. It was the first interurban electric line in the Santa Clara Valley, and it appears to have attracted the interest of both adults and kids posing for this photograph by A.P. Hill. *Courtesy History San José.*

What was this interurban railroad?

In the early twentieth century, with machines of the Industrial Revolution everywhere, roads in California were nevertheless unpaved and automobiles still too costly for the average family. During the transition, the Santa Clara Valley became an early adopter of a transportation innovation that bridged the horse and horsepower. It was the electric interurban railroad.

The first one in the region began construction in 1902 as the San Jose and Los Gatos Interurban Railroad, featuring overhead trolleys to deliver the electric power. It began service in 1903 and was soon joined by two more lines in the Santa Clara Valley. In 1909, the Southern Pacific Railroad—while still operating its own steam-powered trains on a separate line—purchased the three interurban companies and joined them together as the Peninsular Railroad, under the management of Paul Shoup. In 1910, he expanded the Peninsular to include service to Los Altos, Palo Alto, Stanford University and Ravenswood. In Los Altos, the interurban line ran parallel to the SP tracks along what is now Foothill Expressway—the route purchased from Sarah Winchester.

Eventually, there were eighty-one miles of track with hourly service around the valley on a system that carried mostly passengers but also some freight. For a dime, you could travel from Saratoga to Los Gatos or Cupertino to

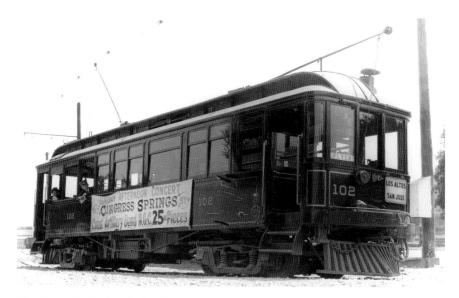

The Peninsular Railroad's Car No. 102. It was a "flyer," meaning it made fewer stops on its route. A banner advertises Congress Springs, then a resort, now a Saratoga Park. *Courtesy Palo Alto Historical Association.*

A 1910 promotional map for the Peninsular sported this bucolic cover. During the spring, the line ran special blossom tours of the Santa Clara Valley. *Courtesy History San José.*

Los Altos. A longer trip—from Palo Alto to San Jose, for example—might cost as much as fifty-five cents.

The electricity came from a main plant in San Jose, with substations in north San Jose, Saratoga and Los Altos. The building that held the Los Altos substation was on First Street and had a second life in the 1950s as the Los Altos Public Library and later housed a local glass company.

The Peninsular rail cars were made of wood and painted a deep red, so the line was sometimes called the "Big Red." Some of the cars featured clerestory roofs—a roof with a sort of skylight— that brought in the California sunshine.

"It was really a beautiful line," says historian Ray Cosyn, who has studied it extensively. "And it was representative of what was happening at that time." Los Angeles, for example, had one thousand miles of interurban track in those days and lines that could take riders to and from cities and villages all over Los Angeles County. Many of the early movie stars in Hollywood, including Charlie Chaplin, wrote about taking their first trips to the studios on those interurban lines.

By 1919, there were ten thousand interurban railway cars in use in the United States and eighteen thousand miles of interurban track. Most of the lines were privately funded by investors.

In the Santa Clara Valley, in order to increase ticket sales, the Peninsular created a stop at Congress Springs, near Saratoga, where there was a park and a hotel. In the spring, when the beauty of the valley's orchards was at its peak, the Peninsular advertised a scenic ride that wended its way through the blossoms. "The greatest of deciduous fruit sections with entrancing valley, foothill, and mountain views," said a Peninsular ad from that era.

Tourists descended on the valley with picnic baskets and hopped off the line—uninvited—to dine and sup in the orchards. In an unpublished memoir, Lyle Job Huestis recalled those scenic tours because, she said, the picnickers often left behind their litter. She remembered her father grumbling as he picked it up from their orchard.

A portion of El Camino Real was paved along the Peninsula in 1912—the first paved road in California. As paving increased and mass production reduced the cost of the automobile, interurban ticket sales declined. The Great Depression of the 1930s dealt another blow, and between 1934 and 1936, the Peninsular Railroad ceased its operations.

Two cars from the Peninsular have been preserved at Solano County's Western Railway Museum. One of them, car No. 52—with a clerestory roof—has been fully restored and is sometimes in use there for transporting visitors.

If you love the idea of electric technology, California innovation and startup companies funded by investors, this is the ticket for you. Visit the Western Railway Museum when you are in that region to see the past's take on the future and catch one more ride on the "Big Red."

Still, that is quite a drive from the Santa Clara Valley. If you want to visit an interurban location that requires a shorter journey, there's always that little railroad stop in the parking lot of the Saratoga Museum.

MORE ABOUT TRAINS AND DEPOTS

For more than a century, it was impossible to get through a single day in the Santa Clara Valley without hearing the whistle of a train. We've already seen that Los Altos came into being when the Southern Pacific bought out Sarah Winchester's land between Palo Alto and Cupertino for its rail line and turned over the surplus for development.

The rails were ubiquitous—both for passengers and freight. "Therefore," wrote historian Eugene Sawyer in 1922, "the orchardists of the valley have easy access to railway transportation." And not just the orchardists. Director Alfred Hitchcock often took the overnight Lark passenger train from his home in Los Angeles to the Santa Clara Valley for easy access to his property in Scotts Valley. Esther Williams took the train from San Francisco down the Peninsula to get married.

By the time Los Altos incorporated in late 1952, the SP line between San Francisco and the Peninsula had become popular with commuters—

The Loyola Corners rail stop, circa 1956—also the era of the estate wagon parked next to it. If you look closely between the rail stop and the wagon, you can see part of the sign for the Echo, a popular local bar. *Courtesy the California State Railroad Museum.*

Though the Southern Pacific tracks and the covered stop at Loyola Corners are both long gone, there is still a Loyola Corners restaurant called Tom's Depot. *Courtesy the California State Railroad Museum.*

Rancho Shopping Center in a vintage postcard from the 1950s. Fremont Avenue ran between the shopping center and the Southern Pacific tracks. In the unpaved area where the cars are parked, there was a covered bench that served as an SP stop. *Author's collection.*

including World War II veterans who moved and made their homes in the Valley of Heart's Delight after the war. A 1947 cartoon-style map by Warren Goodrich, one of the founders of the *Los Altos Town Crier*, features a little railroad track with a steam engine on it, poking along through the village of Los Altos. In the hills above town, he's written a comic alert that cites another long-lost ritual: "Warning! Keep off these roads between 7 & 7:15 a.m.—sleepy wives are driving their husbands to train."

I grew up in Los Altos, and when my father worked in San Francisco, he would walk to Rancho Shopping Center to catch the train. There was a little station there—not a depot—just a covered redwood bench that sat in front of the shopping center.

There was one train going north in the morning and one going south in the evening. And in the evening, when I was on the backyard swing and could swing high enough to see over the old grape stake fence, I could spot the train chugging south near 5:00 p.m. It was, in those days, pulled by an old-fashioned steam engine, which sent up clouds of smoke. When we

spotted it and heard its whistle, we knew Dad would soon be stepping off at the station and walking home with his long stride. When I saw the train, I knew it was time to go inside and wash up for supper.

The big Los Altos depot was downtown at 316 Main Street. Completed in 1913, it was always a beauty and today is a City Historic Landmark. On its debut, the *Palo Alto Times* said the Craftsman-style structure was one of the prettiest on the Peninsula and had "all conveniences, including the latest in drinking fountains." At the peak of rail service, twelve trains a day called there. There was another stop at Loyola Corners, a neighborhood that, thanks to the train, developed into its own unique district. Steps from the little covered-bench station at Loyola Corners there was, for many years, a cocktail longue called the Echo. Maybe it was called that because you could hear the train echoing down the valley from there. Mostly, it was a place where commuters stopped for a little refueling before heading home.

Rail service along this corridor ended in 1962, and though the Echo is long gone, there is still a restaurant at Loyola Corners called Tom's Depot, evoking the train stop that was once the center of that neighborhood. Regional museums in the Santa Clara Valley often salute the old train days with exhibits to remind us of a time when the railroads played a key role in the life of the West. When I visit them, they remind me that the sounds of those trains will always be written on my heart. Sometimes, I can still look back and see my father, forever young, hopping off the Southern Pacific at the Rancho and heading home for dinner in the twilight.

Chapter 5

PARADISE IMPERFECT

Racially restrictive covenants were common practice throughout the United States—yes, including in California—between the 1930s and until well into the 1980s.
—Carol Lynn McKibben

W hen my parents died in 2009 and 2010, I had a great deal of cleaning out to do—as everyone who has ever lost a loved one knows. The family home, their second in the valley, was built in the 1950s, and they had lived there for sixty years. In its cupboards, drawers, closets and attic were files and papers from their long lives. As a journalist and historian, I sorted through the first layer and then set it aside for a time.

One day—and I cannot remember why—I pulled out the original deed to the property on which they built their first home and read it through. If I told you I received a shock, it would be an understatement.

DEED RESTRICTIONS IN THE GOLDEN STATE

There was very little civilian housing built in the United States during World War II. Because of that, it was difficult for my parents to find a home when they moved to California in 1947. My father had been a combat engineer during the war, and once he was reunited with my mother, he resumed his work as an aeronautical engineer and took a job at NACA, the National

Advisory Committee for Aeronautics at Ames Research Center adjacent to what was then Naval Air Station Moffett. NACA was the predecessor of NASA, and its wind tunnel still stands on the edge of Moffett Field, near Mountain View, California.

But civilians couldn't live on the base. The only housing Faye and Ashley Chapman could find back then was a rented room on Emerson Street in Palo Alto, and they shared the kitchen and bathroom. When my older sister was born, things were pretty cramped for a family of three. Acting on a tip from barber Al Galedridge, another World War II veteran who was then working in Palo Alto, my father began looking at lots in nearby Los Altos, where developers were subdividing the orchards.

"Oh, I don't know honey," my mother is reported to have said—according to family lore—when she saw the lot in the apricot orchard near Covington Road. "I'm not sure we want to be this far out in the country."

Ashley talked her into it, bought the lot and a set of plans for a simple cottage-style home and began building it himself on weekends. Most of the work was completed in about eighteen months.

A copy of the deed found in my parents' files for the lot they bought in Santa Clara County that included legal restrictions on what could be done with the property. It also restricted who could live there. *Author's collection.*

Now, I was stunned to read the deed to the land, which came with three pages of restrictions. Most of them were pretty tame. The owners could not live in a trailer. They could not raise farm animals. It was restriction number 5 on the list that was shocking. The property could not be used or occupied, said the deed, "by any persons of African, Japanese, Chinese, Mongolian or Malay descent."

I was stunned to see that in writing.

I knew these ugly, restrictive covenants were common in other parts of the country. I had no idea they had ever been evoked in California—which entered the Union as a free state that outlawed slavery before the Civil War. Los Altos wasn't incorporated until the end of 1952, so I knew this could not be anything imposed by the city.

I was aghast my parents had signed such a thing.

Through a writer friend, I contacted Dr. Carol McKibben, an adjunct professor at Stanford University, who disabused me of the notion that California had been the perfect paradise I had imagined.

"Racially restrictive covenants were common practice throughout the United States—yes, including in California—between the 1930s until well into the 1980s in spite of the Supreme Court Decision, *Shelley v. Kraemer* (1948), which rendered them unenforceable," she wrote me in an email. "They were used to exclude all minorities from predominantly white neighborhoods and even entire towns and cities. In California 'minorities' meant African Americans (especially in large municipalities), Mexicans, and Asians (especially Chinese but also Japanese and Filipinos)," she wrote.

McKibben sent me to the library with the names of several books that filled in the details. I learned these covenants were, in fact, common in the Santa Clara Valley and across the country at that time, beginning with a Federal Housing Authority compromise approved by Congress under President Franklin D. Roosevelt. And although they became unenforceable de jure after the Supreme Court decision in 1948, they still segregated many neighborhoods and communities de facto until (at least) the 1960s. Today, their remnants remain in many homeowners' paperwork—unpleasant reminders of that era.

After I uncovered the story in 2019, I discovered reporter Marisa Kendall of the *San Jose Mercury News* had recently written about this.

"It is really shocking to see the extent they permeated the region," she told me when I reached her. "And it wasn't that long ago they were enforceable."

Some people did stand up against them. Writer Wallace Stegner—a newcomer to California who was looking for a home at about the same time as my parents—resigned from the board of a housing cooperative

A picture of the Chapman home under construction. My father took this photo to send home to his parents, and as you can see, he also captured his shadow. *Author's collection.*

when restrictive covenants were proposed there. At about the same time, the United Autoworkers Union and the American Friends Service Committee fought for unrestricted housing in Milpitas and Mountain View. Both efforts were initially unsuccessful; but change did come—eventually.

In the 1950s, Bay Area builder Joseph Eichler, a man born in 1900 into a traditional Jewish family, refused to allow restrictive covenants on deeds of his homes, insisting all his developments be open to all. With a stand like that and changes in federal law, the barriers began to come down.

Which led me back to my own feelings about my parents and the deed I discovered.

Writer Jan Batiste Adkins is the friend I first called when I began researching this story. We met initially because we share the same publisher. She specializes in writing about the African American experience in the San Francisco Bay Area. The day I called her, I was in distress about what I had uncovered in my family's story.

First, she gave me sources to help in my research, and that is always a gift.

Then, she told me to have compassion for my parents, who lived in a different time and faced pressures unknown to me.

"You don't know what was in their hearts," she said.

What a lesson this was in the power of forgiveness. From family papers, I learned an unpleasant history.

From a friend, I gained a lesson in tolerance.

African American Contributions

Sam McDonald was born in Louisiana, the grandchild of slaves, and was six years old when his family moved to California in 1890. When his parents made plans to move to Oregon, he left home at sixteen and worked on a Sacramento River steamboat.

In 1903, McDonald moved to Mayfield—the early Palo Alto townsite—and found a job at Stanford University, where he would work the rest of his life. He began as a night watchman and eventually rose to become superintendent of buildings and grounds. During his half century at the university, he raised thousands of dollars for what was then called Stanford's Home for Convalescent Children with an annual cookout he organized. In addition, Sam McDonald also quietly helped underwrite the college expenses of an untold number of students.

McDonald never married. His autobiography, *Sam McDonald's Farm*, was copyrighted under his birth name, Emanuel B. McDonald, and was

Sam McDonald organized annual cookouts on the Stanford campus to help raise money for what was then called Stanford's Home for Convalescent Children. *Courtesy Stanford University Slide Collection (PC0141).*

published by Stanford University Press in 1954. When he died in 1957, the university discovered he had been both thrifty and wise in his investments and was the owner of a four-hundred-acre ranch near La Honda, where he had built a lodge and spent his free time. In his will, he deeded the property to Stanford.

In 1958, San Mateo County purchased the land from Stanford and set it aside as a park. The county has now doubled it in size. It is a lovely place of trails that wind through redwood forests and open meadows. What a remarkable story this land tells of one man's journey in California.

I discovered the tale in a book by Jan Batiste Adkins, whom I mentioned previously. She's the author of *African Americans of San Jose and Santa Clara County*, published by Arcadia in 2019.

"These early pioneers, seeking the land of dreams, faced overwhelming obstacles with courage," Adkins writes. Another reminder that the Santa Clara Valley was not always a paradise of equality for all.

Among these pioneers: the maternal grandfather of Juana Briones, Philipe (sometimes written as Felipe or Felix) Santiago Tapia, a man of African and Spanish descent, who was one of the first of the Spanish-speaking civilian immigrants to settle in what became Santa Clara County.

McDonald's four-hundred-acre ranch in the Santa Cruz Mountains was later purchased by San Mateo County and is now a public park. *Photo by Robin Chapman.*

In her book, Adkins also features Mary Edmonia Lewis, the first African American sculptor to achieve international fame. Her works are now on display in the California Room of the Dr. Martin Luther King Jr. Library in San Jose.

Looking back at these lives, and many others Jan writes about, it is meaningful to ponder the struggles and triumphs of those who worked to ensure America fulfilled—and fulfills today—its promise to all. Citizens should not have to fight to obtain the rights granted to them by God and codified in our law. Yet so many persevered.

It is another good reason—besides the redwoods—to hike the trails in Sam McDonald Park and remember.

WALTER SINGER'S JOURNEY

Walter Singer died in 1992, which isn't an especially long time ago. But it has been long enough for many in the Santa Clara Valley to have lost the thread of his story. He faced up to some big sorrows in his lifetime yet did so without rancor. His story deserves to be remembered.

During his lifetime, he was so active in local organizations and so loved and admired in his adopted hometown that people affectionately called him "Mr. Los Altos." Following his untimely death, civic leaders dedicated a sculpture to him in the newly remodeled Community Plaza. The bronze bust, created by artist Ingrid Jackson-MacDonald, is now listed on the Smithsonian Art inventory of sculpture in public places.

Or at least it was, when the sculpture was in a public place.

In 2014, the Los Altos City Council voted to remodel the plaza and remove the Walter Singer bronze. Council member Jarrett Fishpaw, twenty-seven years old, may have spoken for many residents when he said, "I walked in Community Plaza most of my life without a single trace or clue as to the impact the gentleman immortalized there had on the community." Context is critical in public art. In just two decades, a community had forgotten the story of one of its heroes.

Singer was born in Germany in 1923, the son of a Lutheran mother and a Jewish father. In 1935, Nazi laws stripped Jews of their citizenship and outlawed marriage between Jews and non-Jews. The Singers were now in danger. In 1939, after Walter's father was arrested, Walter and his mother fled to San Francisco with the help of a cousin. The dangers of Nazi rule often split immigrant families, another cruelty suffered even by those who survived.

"I arrived pretty much with the clothes on my back," Singer said in an oral history in the archives of the Los Altos History Museum. "An extra set of underwear, an extra pair of shoes and $4 in my pocket."

His mother found work cleaning houses. A friend told them about Frank and Josephine Duveneck of the Santa Clara Valley, a philanthropic couple who might help. When Mrs. Duveneck visited the Singers in San Francisco and saw their tiny living quarters, she went into action. Within an hour, she had bundled Walter into her blue Ford for the drive down the Peninsula to the Duveneck home at Hidden Villa in the rural landscape that became Los Altos Hills.

At the Duvenecks' dining room table, the sixteen-year-old began to flourish.

The bronze bust of Walter Singer had pride of place in a plaza at the entrance to Los Altos for twenty years. He always wore very big eyeglasses, just like the ones on the bronze. *Photo by Robin Chapman.*

"I wanted some more potatoes and asked for them in German," he recalled, "and nothing happened. They made me learn English, which was the best thing that ever happened to me in my life."

Eager to learn more, Singer enrolled in Palo Alto High School, heading down the hill each morning with the Duvenecks' son Bernard in his car.

After graduation and two years at Golden Gate University, he enlisted in the U.S. Army, going back to Europe to serve as a translator near the end of World War II. When the war was over, he and his mother learned his father had died in a Nazi concentration camp.

Singer became an American citizen, found a job and, at a dance in San Carlos, met Marie Ohanian, who became his wife. The couple wed at Hidden Villa. They moved to Los Altos Hills in 1961 and in 1976 purchased Los Altos Stationers, located in the building on Main Street now occupied by a bakery and restaurant.

After their teenage daughter was killed by a drunken driver, Singer turned to a life of service. At the Rotary Club, the Los Altos Village Association, the United Way and the Chamber of Commerce, he volunteered. As one of the founders of the Festival of Lights Parade in Los Altos, it was Singer who climbed aboard a float each year to serve as Santa Claus.

In 1989, he got shattering news. He had contracted AIDS from a tainted blood transfusion during heart surgery. He was stunned and afraid.

Before his illness, Singer was instrumental in organizing a local Christmas parade and played Santa Claus on one of the floats. Here he embraces his wife, Marie, circa 1980. *Courtesy the* Los Altos Town Crier.

"I didn't tell anyone besides my wife and son," he said, "because of the stigma attached to AIDS."

Several months later, fearing the reaction of his customers, he quietly sold his business, saying he and his wife had decided to retire.

In the meantime, Singer heard about a fellow Rotarian, former Los Altos High School principal Dushan "Dude" Angius, whose son had contracted AIDS and had come home to his family to die. Singer confided in Angius and learned about something Angius had initiated called the Rotary AIDS Project.

"I told him he would feel much better—and might help a lot of other people—if he would talk about it," Angius told me in 2014 when he was eighty-six. Angius was my high school principal, and we had stayed in touch.

"After six months of vacillating back and forth," Singer said later, "I decided to go public."

When he took the podium at the December 7, 1989 Rotary Club meeting, only Angius and one other friend knew what he planned to say.

"I'm going to talk to you today about a matter of life and death," he began as a hush fell over the crowd and he choked back tears.

When he stopped speaking, "every member, some crying, some unable to speak, came up and gave me a hug," he said. "I had asked my fellow Rotarians if they would be my support group, and they came through 100 percent."

In return, he spent the remaining years of his life educating others about the egalitarian nature of AIDS. In the 1980s, people who were diagnosed with the disease faced a death sentence and a public that frequently shut them out. Singer worked to change that. He spoke to dozens and dozens of organizations.

His story went national and then international—from the *CBS Morning News* to headlines in more than four hundred newspapers. He took a featured role in the Rotary Club's *Los Altos Story*, a Peabody Award–winning documentary seen by millions worldwide.

"It's not taboo to talk about AIDS anymore," said Jane Reed, Rotarian, former mayor and past president of the board of the Los Altos History Museum. "We have people like Walter Singer to thank for that."

Singer was sixty-eight years old when he died in 1992. His funeral—presided over by both a rabbi and a Protestant minister—drew an overflow crowd of mourners. A year later, the city he loved dedicated the bronze tribute to him in a small downtown plaza, and hundreds more people turned

The bronze tribute to Singer was completed before his death. Here, the man meets the statue. Photo by Joe Melena. *Courtesy the* Los Altos Town Crier.

out for the ceremony. Singer had been able to see a model of the bronze before he died.

Singer's journey continued, in a way, even after his death. When the tribute was removed in 2014, it was placed in storage in the utility barn at the Los Altos History Museum. Singer, a Holocaust survivor and World War II veteran, had his bronze removed to make more room in a park that had just been renamed Veterans Plaza.

None of this takes anything away from his story.

"Walter was a giver," Dude Angius told me a short time before his own death in 2017—an apt summary of Walter Singer's life.

Repeatedly, he chose service to others and gratitude. Bronze statue aside— and we have seen in the twenty-first century how these come and go—this is Walter Singer's lasting legacy.

TRIBUTE TO A TEACHER AND FRIEND

I don't know exactly when I decided to become a journalist, but I do remember the first person who told me I could do it.

I was a student in high school, and one spring, I joined the staff of the *Lance*, our biweekly newspaper. Our adviser was a young teacher, not long out of what was then Chico State College. Her name was Marlene Maselli— later Marlene Schuessler. She was a mentor and friend for many decades.

She died on Easter Sunday in 2020, at the height of the Covid pandemic, after a yearlong battle with cancer. There was no funeral, as large gatherings were prohibited. Since we couldn't pay tribute to her in a celebration of life, I thought I might tell you a little about her and what a difference she made in mine.

In her class, long ago, I learned all the fundamentals of news, from writing headlines to meeting deadlines. These were the tools I used when I went to work as a journalist in several major cities, including San Francisco and Washington, D.C.

Tools are important. But it was her encouragement that changed my life. My parents were quiet people, and they were careful with their praise. Miss Maselli was generous with hers. After just one semester in her class, this is what she wrote in my yearbook: "It's too difficult to include all of the accolades that I would like to include—but here goes! You're great Robin— that's it!" She then listed what she felt were my talents in her friendly, looping handwriting.

Teacher Marlene Maselli and her soon-to-be husband, Duane Schuessler, looking young and in love about 1970. *Courtesy of Duane Schuessler and Gina Jackson.*

What a wow this was to an insecure teenager. I often think of all the students she must have lifted up during her long career in education. She had a huge smile and seemed to beam her way through life as she moved up at the district, married husband Duane, settled into her Los Altos home and nurtured her daughter Gina. In the last years of her life, she spoke with great joy of her presidentially named grandchildren: Andrew, Truman, Reagan and Madison. Their father works for the governor of Nebraska. Too far away, she often said; but she was not yet ready to leave her native California, so she and Duane traveled frequently from Los Gatos to the Cornhusker State.

Her grandfather was an immigrant from Italy who produced olive oil in the Central Valley. I knew she loved California history, so I dedicated my first book of Santa Clara Valley history to her. When I learned she was gone, I didn't know what to do, so, fighting tears, I went for a walk. On my route, the answer struck me: I must write about her, of course. She would have encouraged it. In fact, I think she did.

ONE MAN'S PANDEMIC

Richard Abbott is a World War II veteran and the father of a girl I knew in my hometown who was a few years ahead of me in high school. She died of cancer far too young. Her father, born in 1922, had many more years remaining to him after he lost her. Born at the end of the flu pandemic that swept the world near the end of World War I, he lived to see the Covid-19 pandemic almost a century later. In 2020, he watched as Union Presbyterian in Los Altos, his local church for more than five decades, struggled to celebrate Christmas with remote services and a socially distanced, outdoor caroling event on Christmas Eve. In October of that year, Dick Abbott celebrated his ninety-eighth birthday.

Shortly afterward, he came down with what he thought was a bad cold. He went to the Veterans' Hospital in Palo Alto to double check, tested positive for the Covid-19 virus and was admitted to the hospital. This was not good news for a man of his years.

Yet, after just four days he had improved so much he was discharged from the hospital and sent home to recuperate. Dick Abbott made a full recovery and was happy to pose wearing his favorite Christmas sweater for an article on his Christmas miracle. When Union Presbyterian Church began celebrating its services again in person in 2021, there was Dick Abbott, in his usual pew.

"The doctors at the VA were so surprised, they paid me to be part of a study," he says with a smile, recalling his recovery from a virus that seemed

Richard Abbott at the age of ninety-eight in a photo taken at Christmas 2020, after he had survived his bout with the Covid-19 virus. *Photo by Robin Chapman.*

to be especially hard on people over sixty-five years of age—an age more than three decades in his rearview mirror. He has twin siblings, by the way, who also live in the Bay Area and who are both in their nineties. Very good DNA in the Abbott family.

He has been a member of Union Church since 1958, still serves as a deacon and still drives his own car, "but only about five miles a week," he laughs. In fact, during the pandemic he renewed his California driver's license, and it doesn't expire until he is 103 years old.

PANDEMIC PANACEA

The Covid-19 pandemic was definitely a challenge for the Santa Clara Valley, not to mention the world. Many of us had a lot of trouble thinking of a bright side to a long experience that made some people sick, took far too many lives and isolated so many. But there was one small thing on the positive side: those Little Free Libraries scattered around neighborhoods kept a lot of us from losing our minds when we were quarantined and our public libraries were closed. You take a book or leave a book. No paperwork necessary. Invented by Tod Bol of Wisconsin, they are now all over the world.

In one, I found something special.

It was the novel *Miss Buncle Married* by a writer I'd never heard of called D.E. Stevenson. It was a modern edition of a 1936 book, and its author, Dorothy Emily Stevenson (1892–1973), I discovered, was a first cousin, once removed, of Robert Louis Stevenson. During her lifetime, she was a best-selling author who wrote forty novels and sold more than seven million copies of her books worldwide.

Known as DES, she grew up in Edinburgh and as a child was discouraged by her family from becoming a writer like her cousin. Her father, David Alan Stevenson, first cousin to RLS and a lighthouse engineer in the family firm, refused to send his daughter to university, saying he did not want a bluestocking—that is, an intellectual woman—in the family.

But as she later wrote, "My head was full of stories and they got lost if I did not write them down."

When I learned of her familial connections to RLS, I contacted Mitchell Manson, a retired geneticist who is president of the RLS Club of Edinburgh and whom I had met through the Robert Louis Stevenson Club of Monterey. He did not know about DES but discovered there was a plaque in his

Above: This Little Free Library sits in front of a residence in the Santa Clara Valley. Each one is unique. All provide a great way to circulate used books. *Photo by Robin Chapman.*

Right: Dorothy Emily Stevenson (1892–1973) lived the conventional life of an upper-middle-class wife and mother. She also wrote best-selling novels, and she appears to have enjoyed the fun. *Courtesy Robert Louis Stevenson Club of Edinburgh, Scotland.*

hometown of Edinburgh in her honor. Was it nature or nurture, I asked him, that produced two such successful authors in two generations of the same family? He pointed out that Dorothy's relationship to RLS—first cousin, once removed—meant she would have shared just 6.25 percent of his DNA.

"Not very much," he said. "But then perhaps just enough to share some characteristics."

Miss Buncle Married turned out to be a deft comedy of manners that takes place in a fictional English village and reads a bit like Jane Austen—if Austen's books had been co-authored by a humorist like P.G. Wodehouse, of Bertie Wooster and Jeeves fame. The book is a novel about a woman who writes a novel about a woman who writes a novel: "sort of like a recurring decimal," says one of the characters. It was so funny, at one point I had to set it down because I was laughing so hard I could no longer see. I discovered I was reading a sequel and went back and read the first book, *Miss Buncle's Book*, and found it equally charming and also very funny.

Perhaps it isn't any wonder that half a century after her death, DES is still a much-loved author. More than forty of her titles are available in print and digital form, and like her cousin RLS, she has inspired clubs around the world of her fans.

Being transported by a book put me in mind of a quote from the scholar Erasmus, who famously said, "When I get a little money, I buy books. If any is left, I buy food and clothes."

The Little Free Library goes Erasmus one better: no charge for the books and a moveable feast for the restless reader.

Chapter 6

SERVICE

There are more than twice as many American Legion posts
in the U.S. today as there are Walmarts.
—Paul E. Dillard

Moffett Field features prominently in this chapter, and that's because Moffett Federal Airfield has played a big part in the life of the Santa Clara Valley since its opening in 1933. Historic Hangar One is there, one of the largest unsupported, freestanding structures in the world and a key landmark in our region. It is so big pilots like to say—and this may be apocryphal—it has its own weather, with fog and precipitation sometimes appearing inside the hangar. Before I reported this was true, I would call a meteorologist.

When my parents died, I discovered in their papers a lifetime family membership to the Moffett Field Historical Society and Museum. After I reached for a hankie, I drove out there, told the folks at the museum my parents' lifetime memberships had expired and asked if I could buy one of my own.

Not all the stories in this chapter are about Moffett. But they are all about service. And we do begin at Moffett Field.

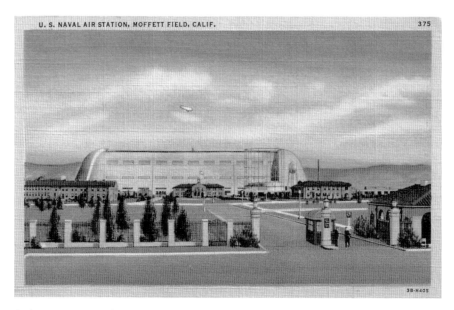

A vintage postcard of Moffett Field sent in the final year of World War II. *Author's collection.*

SWEETHEART JEWELRY

Diana Parsons, secretary of the Moffett Field Historical Society and Museum, can remember exactly when she saw her first piece of military sweetheart jewelry.

She was five years old and traveling by bus with her mother to California. During the journey, a kind lady took the squirmy child on her lap, and Parsons found herself transfixed by a pin the woman was wearing. It was in the shape of a tiny spoon and had a U.S. Navy emblem on its handle.

Before the long bus ride ended, the stranger had given the pin to the child, and Parsons—without quite realizing it—had begun her collection of military sweetheart jewelry. It is now on display at the Moffett museum.

"The tradition of sending jewelry mementoes home to loved ones began during World War I," says Parsons, whose husband, Harold "Herb" Parsons, is a navy veteran and president of the Moffett museum. "But it intensified during World War II, when more than sixteen million Americans served. These jewelry pieces were a reminder of family members far from home and a public way to express patriotism."

On display at the museum are "V for Victory" pins covered in red, white and blue stones; earrings in the shape of B-24 bombers; and bracelets, lockets, cufflinks, sweater pins, compacts and charms all featuring the insignias of the various branches of the service.

Some pieces represent U.S. allies, including a World War II bracelet sporting the flags of France, China, Britain and the Soviet Union—one of the rare times in history we have seen those flags joined together. Another piece is engraved with the haunting names of World War I battlefields—Reims, Verdun, Soissons and Saint-Mihiel—the panels linked with tiny crosses of Lorraine. One pin is made from the tunic button of a Royal Canadian Air Force uniform and is encircled with a silver wreath of remembrance. Was the flyer lost? We cannot know, but it is poignant still.

Each piece has a story. The ones engraved with "Mother" and "Beloved Wife" are easily deciphered. But what to make of the silver bracelet with the U.S. Navy insignia that is engraved with the names of nine different girls? Big family? Many ports?

The jewelry is always on display at the museum, but it becomes especially popular around Valentine's Day. Although few of the pieces are made of

Some of the sweetheart jewelry on display at the Moffett Field Historical Society Museum. The bracelet listing World War I battles is at the bottom of the photo. Diana Parson's very first spoon-shaped pin is at left. *Photo by Robin Chapman.*

valuable materials or studded with expensive stones, each, long ago, had immeasurable value to a loved one. Each is now a piece of history that once linked the battlefront to those who served at home.

Visit the museum, in the shadow of Hangar One, and ask for Diana Parsons. If she is available, she will be happy to show you something very special: the little pin in the shape of a spoon that pleased a child one day and started a collection.

THE POWER OF ARTIFACTS

Historical artifacts travel a curious road as they move from the jewelry boxes and closets of the living to the glass cases of museums.

"These objects are links between past and present," said retired U.S. Navy Rear Admiral James Schear, who spoke at a 2018 ceremony at the Moffett Field Historical Society and Museum that featured the dedication of a new display honoring Rear Admiral William A. Moffett, after whom Moffett Naval Air Station was named. It includes his military sword and a duplicate of his Medal of Honor, awarded to him for valor in 1914.

A duplicate Medal of Honor is rare, but because the original rests in the vaults of the Naval Aviation Museum in Pensacola, Florida, and is not on display, the duplicate, awarded by the United States Navy Awards Board at the Pentagon, will enable visitors to connect with the admiral as a hero decorated by President Woodrow Wilson, not just as a man who was an able military administrator.

The sword also has a backstory. U.S. Marine Colonel Bill Moffett, grandson of the admiral, played with it as a child and later found it in his father's belongings after his death. He was not sure the sword

Rear Admiral William A. Moffett was awarded the Medal of Honor in 1914 for his bravery under fire in the siege of Veracruz. This duplicate is on display at the Moffett Museum. *Photo by Robin Chapman.*

My grandfather Joseph Roy Chapman was
a World War I veteran. His photograph was
used in the Santa Clara Valley to localize
a U.S. Archives traveling exhibit honoring
the 100th anniversary of the end of the war.
Personal images like this can help us in the
twenty-first century relate to these milestones
of the past. *Author's collection.*

was genuine, since the etching on the blade misspells his grandfather's
middle name. The sword is engraved with the middle name spelled "Adgar,"
though the admiral's middle name is "Adger." Moffett museum president
Herb Parsons knew about this spelling error from his research. He was able
to authenticate the sword and add it to the museum's collection.

Admiral Moffett, the first chief of the navy's Bureau of Aeronautics, died
with seventy-two others when the rigid airship USS *Akron* went down off the
coast of New Jersey on April 4, 1933. The airfield was named in his honor.

The Los Altos History Museum has often enriched its exhibits with local
military artifacts, adding them to one traveling exhibit from the National
Archives marking the 100th anniversary of the end of World War I.

"Objects last longer than we do, so they bear witness," says Elizabeth
Ward, the museum's director. "It is a magical thing to encounter an object a
century old—something really special happens between object and viewer."

One object on display: a carefully crafted U.S. officer's uniform cap
molded in brass from a discarded shell casing. The work, possibly created
in the trenches of World War I or by an artisan at a nearby farmhouse,
transformed the remains of a deadly explosive into a souvenir. It has an
emotional resonance as a reminder of an unknown soldier and unknown
craftsman. Even its resonance has changed over the years as the object
moved from shell casing to memento to twenty-first-century museum object.

These items were once part of the lives of people long ago and are now
the only remaining witnesses to days of great danger and great change.

On the Wings of Eagles

After I bought my lifetime membership in the Moffett Field Historical Society and Museum, I began entering their annual drawing for a free ride on a World War II aircraft. The drawing was part of the regular visits of the Collings Foundation's "Wings of Freedom Tour," which had been bringing vintage military aircraft to Moffett since 1999. In 2019, Herb Parsons from the museum called to say I had won the drawing and could pick a bomber for my free flight.

I had mixed feelings about this. I wanted to take advantage of the opportunity, but I confess to being frightened to go aloft in one of these antiquated aircraft. "What happens if I pass up on this?" I asked Herb. "Do you save any money?" "No," he replied. "We just give it to somebody else." I said I would do it.

My flight happened to coincide with the seventy-fifth anniversary of Operation Overlord, the Allied invasion of Europe that took place on June 6, 1944—the largest invasion by sea in history. Once I decided I would write about this flight to commemorate D-Day, I began to think of it as a news assignment, and I had flown in lots of aircraft on assignment as a reporter. Working on it as a job served to table my fears, and I knew D-Day still had the power to resonate with readers.

"I remember it well," said Chester "Chet" Clark, eighty-two years old when I interviewed him at Moffett in 2019. "I was seven years old then, and I used to sit on my father's lap and read the war news with him. I remember asking him what the 'D' meant."

For the record, the letter "D" was a military placeholder for the chosen day—a day kept secret as the Allies prepared to launch their attack against Hitler's war machine. I met Clark as we sat together at Moffett, waiting to fly in restored World War II aircraft. It was Clark's third such flight and my first. He was going up in a P-40 Warhawk. I was catching a ride in a B-24 Liberator called "Witchcraft."

The B-24 was certainly imposing to look at. But after I crawled inside and we hulked into the air, it felt cramped and slow. With modern Silicon Valley spread out below, it seemed astonishing America had won a war with these lumbering machines. The aircraft I was in had not been modified for passengers. We were told to be careful walking around the bomb bay doors because if we stepped on them, we could fall out. "And don't touch anything that is painted red," said the man who briefed us. "That might be dangerous." After the briefing, one guy on the ride found a bench seat

That's me, giving the thumbs-up in front of the B-24 Liberator at Moffett Field. I'm showing much more bravado than I felt. *Author's collection.*

behind the pilot and said, "Don't touch me. I'm not moving an inch during this flight." I was told to sit on the floor and buckle my safety belt for takeoff.

On D-Day, the Allies filled the skies with ten thousand propeller-driven aircraft like the B-24 in which I flew. Lots of crews during the war did not survive. Others had to bail out over France and Germany and spent the war in Nazi prison camps.

Not all the aircraft on D-Day brought death. The late Colonel Douglas A. Riach of California landed on Omaha Beach as a first lieutenant on D-Day, serving with the 116th Infantry Regiment of the 29th Infantry Division. He made it as far as Vierville before he was wounded on the advance toward St. Lo by a "Bouncing Betty" mine. Medics took him to the beach on the hood of a Jeep, and the crew of a rescue aircraft from across the English Channel flew him to safety and a British hospital. He recovered to rejoin his unit as it crossed the Rhine. His story is recounted in a book I found in my father's library, *World War II Reminiscences*, published by the Reserve Officers Association of California.

Today, we think of the successful outcome of D-Day as a foregone conclusion, but it did not feel that way at the time. Local resident Ruth

Looking out the window of the B-24 and down on modern Silicon Valley. With a sunny sky above and peace and prosperity below, it was hard to imagine that men had flown these slow, fragile machines under fire. *Photo by Robin Chapman.*

Dorney was ninety-five years old when I interviewed her about D-Day. She said she first heard the news of it in New York, as she celebrated her college graduation with two friends.

"They both had loved ones overseas," she remembered. "We listened to the early reports on the radio, and it was a tense time."

Three-quarters of a century later, my B-24 flight took us over the Apple campus in Cupertino and on to peaceful Los Gatos and back. Yet that short journey brought to mind the brave souls who once flew these aircraft under fire. Today, most of us only know these bombers from old movies. Now, for me, the distinctive sound of their big piston engines will always evoke the courage of those who risked their lives to help hasten the end of a terrible war.

TRAGEDY

I was lucky in more ways than one to have caught that flight on "Witchcraft" in 2019. As it turns out, it was not unreasonable to have been apprehensive about flying in such an old aircraft.

In October 2019, just a few months after I took my flight, the Collings Foundation's B-17G Flying Fortress "Nine O Nine" was lost in a crash at Bradley International Airport in Windsor Locks, Connecticut. Seven of the thirteen people on board were killed, including the pilot, Ernest "Mac" McCauley, seventy-five, the most experienced B-17 pilot in the world, whom I chatted with in the crew lounge at Moffett that June. Six others, including one person on the ground, were injured. The aircraft itself was destroyed.

The accident served to suspend the Collings Foundation's tours and may have ended them entirely.

It was a tragedy on many levels. The families of the victims are grieving. The Collings Foundation has also been devastated. Its "Wings of Freedom" mission was to educate people about the role these aircraft played in bringing the deadliest war in history to an end.

Collings supported its work by selling rides. The foundation almost immediately found another B-17 and began restoring it and hoped to quickly rebound. But the Federal Aviation Administration withdrew Collings's Living History Flight Exemption—which allowed the not-for-profit to carry passengers on the aging fleet—while the National Transportation Safety Board investigated. The final investigation report blamed pilot error and inadequate maintenance for the crash.

The B-17G Flying Fortress "Nine O Nine" visiting Moffett Field in May 2019, when I captured it in this photo. Five months later, it was destroyed in a crash. *Photo by Robin Chapman.*

The Moffett Field Historical Society and Museum had long benefited from the Collings tour. For twenty years, crowds came to Moffett to see the Collings aircraft and then stopped into the museum while they were there. Museum volunteers staffed tables outside, and it was prime time for fundraising.

Members of the public are also victims. As we lose veterans of the Greatest Generation, the memory of their deeds grows dim. Chet Clark, the man I met who was waiting to catch a ride in a P-30 Warhawk the same day I was going up, remembered hearing about D-Day as a child—air cover provided by the propeller-driven wonders we saw at Moffett. Clark is among a small number of Americans alive today who still have a memory of D-Day.

With many in the region, I mourn with the families of the victims of the Collings tragedy. And I will miss seeing those historic American machines.

SMALL STEPS AND GIANT LEAPS

NASA Ames Research Center at Moffett Field played an important role in mankind's first landing on the moon on July 20, 1969. Santa Clara Valley resident Henry "Hank" Cole, born in 1921, worked on the Apollo program at NASA Ames that helped send Neil Armstrong, Buzz Aldrin and Michael Collins to the moon and put mankind's first footprints on the lunar surface.

I wrote this story for the fiftieth anniversary of Apollo 11 in 2019 and had a chance to chat with Cole when he was ninety-eight years old and very busy helping NASA with its research for the anniversary celebration. My editor, Bruce Barton, had found Cole's oral history online, and I tracked the busy engineer to his home in the valley and spent a delightful morning chatting with him.

Cole has a love of aeronautics that goes back to his childhood in Washington State, a time when, as he puts it, "aviation was just getting started" and the idea of space flight was the stuff of science fiction.

As a high school senior in Tacoma, Cole began building model airplanes. Unlike other teens, he was not content to just build them. He began designing airfoils for them—that is, finding better ways to speed them through the air using the science of flight. At the public library, he discovered airfoil reports from an obscure federal think tank called the National Advisory Committee for Aeronautics or NACA—an agency that would one day become NASA—

Henry "Hank" Cole in 2019 at the age of ninety-eight with his dog Mimmi. Cole truly loves being an aeronautical engineer. *Photo by Robin Chapman.*

Hank Cole, in 1959, showing the award-winning HC-9 Wakefield radio-controlled model plane he built in his spare time. *Courtesy Hank Cole.*

and he was fascinated. He decided to study aeronautical engineering at the University of Washington.

Cole completed his studies, but World War II intervened and kept him from further research for the duration of the war. As a naval officer and engineer serving on the aircraft carrier USS *Nehenta Bay* (CVE-74), he survived eight battles in the Pacific, working to keep his squadron's aircraft aloft in combat that he still does not like to talk about.

When the war ended, the GI Bill helped him return to the University of Washington for graduate school, where he became friends with fellow student Scott Crossfield, who, as a test pilot in 1953, would become the first man to top pilot Chuck Yeager and fly twice the speed of sound. As a reporter in Washington, D.C., I once had the opportunity to interview Crossfield at the Smithsonian's National Air and Space Museum.

Cole's journey brought him in 1951 to California, where he joined Crossfield at the agency he had once read about in his local library—the NACA Ames Research Center at Moffett Field. On NACA trips to Edwards Air Force Base in Southern California, Cole said Crossfield and another test pilot "used to fly us around." The other pilot was a quiet fellow by the name of Neil Armstrong.

"I never would have guessed he would go to the moon," Cole said of Armstrong. "He was, I wouldn't say shy, but reserved. He didn't say anything without thinking about it. And he was a very good pilot."

In the evenings, Cole played ping pong with the pilots and discovered how competitive they were. Cole had been a ping pong champion in college, but he found the future astronauts impossible to beat.

He joined the space race when NACA became NASA—the National Aeronautics and Space Administration—established by President Dwight D. Eisenhower in 1958. Cole began to work with the Ames model shop to build rocket and spacecraft models they could test in the wind tunnel.

One day, the legendary and controversial Wernher von Braun—who once built rockets for Hitler and who survived to serve with NASA—asked Cole's boss, Smith J. DeFrance, to have his team test two proposed Apollo Saturn launch vehicles.

"It is a good thing we did that," Cole said. "We discovered two important things. When a spacecraft was transonic—crossing the sound barrier—there was less buffeting if the craft approached at an angle. Also, one of the rockets they gave us to test had a flaw and would have blown up."

Cole's life has been rich in experience. Although he lost his wife in 2015, his son Matthew lives with him and his daughter Marina visits often. He doesn't remember everything he and his family were doing on that day more than fifty years ago when he and the rest of the world watched Neil Armstrong and Buzz Aldrin walk on the moon.

But he will always remember the day itself. On July 20, 1969, the Cole family was celebrating. Not just the successful moon landing up there, 238,900 miles in space, a landing in which Hank Cole had played his part; but another giant leap closer to home. That was the day Cole's daughter Marina took her first small steps on planet Earth.

FLYING OUT OF NUQ

Even though Moffett Naval Air Station was decommissioned in the 1990s, the airfield at Moffett remains a federal facility. When the president of the United States or the vice president comes to Silicon Valley, Air Force One and Air Force Two nearly always land at Moffett Field. The field carries the international code NUQ.

Because of its federal designation, Moffett has played host to a range of important aircraft since it was completed in 1933, from the navy rigid airship USS *Macon* once based at Hangar One, to the Blue Angels, who used to perform for Bay Area events out of Moffett (until the Naval Air Station was decommissioned), to today's Google fleet, which has access to the field through a long-term lease on part of the old base. Actor James Stewart earned his U.S. Army Air Corps wings at Moffett when pilots were training there before America entered World War II and then flew combat missions in the war. During the Cold War, Moffett was home to the navy's P-3 Orions, whose squadrons hunted Russian submarines in the Pacific. As tensions eased after 1989, NUQ also hosted a civil aviation flying club. My father, a retired army reserve officer, and his friend Oliver Frasier—both Alabama natives and World War II veterans—joined the flying club at NUQ and flew together for fun.

In March 1987, when I was home on a visit from my reporting job in the East, my dad and Ollie Frasier offered to take me with them on a flight from Moffett to Monterey, the only time I have ever had a chance to fly with my father. It seemed like a great idea.

However, all during the flight over the Santa Cruz Mountains, my father was jumpy. He was piloting the aircraft, and Ollie was in the copilot's seat. I

My father shared a Cessna with fellow World War II veteran Oliver Frasier, who had flown over France on D-Day. I took this photograph of my dad going over his preflight checklist the day he and Fraser flew me to Monterey. *Photo by Robin Chapman.*

was somewhat alarmed when my father kept squirming, as if he were looking for a way out of the plane. At one point, he even used a swear word—very unusual for my father, especially in the presence of a lady. Egad, I thought: I wonder how my mother will handle losing both of us in one day?

When we did touch down at MRY—Monterey Regional Airport—my father was sheepish. It seems he had changed the batteries in his audio headset just before takeoff, placing the old batteries in the back pocket of his trousers. The batteries were apparently not yet dead and during the flight kept making contact with his keys, creating an electric arc that gave him repeated shocks to his derrière.

After my father died in 2010, I found his pilot's logbook and looked up the entry for the date we flew and had a good laugh remembering our trip. A number of pages later, I spotted something else interesting.

On September 9, 1993, he and a friend made a flight to Livermore—LVK in the international airport code—and on the way back, as he noted in his log, he "heard AF1 get landing clearance @ NUQ," adding, "Saw AF1 and AF2 on the apron." By AF1 and AF2, he meant Air Force One and Air Force Two, the aircraft that carry the two most important people in the executive branch of our government.

A check in the news archives confirms President Bill Clinton and Vice President Al Gore were in the Santa Clara Valley on that day for a meeting in Sunnyvale. Each, as is standard operating procedure, was flying in his own designated Air Force plane, not flying together for what is known as "continuity of government" reasons.

My father, in his Cessna 152, was a taxpayer who loved aeronautics. From his log, it is clear he got quite a charge out of seeing two of our nation's most awe-inspiring aircraft landing right there on his home field.

And this time, he did not need any stray batteries to add to the thrill.

Camp Fremont and the 1918 Pandemic

During the 1918–19 influenza pandemic, the Santa Clara Valley faced many of the same issues California residents faced during the Covid-19 pandemic. But a century ago, locals had an added complication: World War I's Camp Fremont on rural acreage in Palo Alto and Menlo Park had just begun training nearly thirty thousand soldiers to join the American Expeditionary Force in France.

As writer Barbara Wilcox discovered in researching her book *The Story of Camp Fremont* (2016), barracks, tents, mess halls and parade grounds proved to be an ideal environment for the virus to spread. As soldiers moved within their ranks and then around the nation and the world, the virus and the death it carried moved with them.

This pandemic from the previous century is believed to have first appeared in the United States near an army base in Kansas. The first case in the Santa Clara Valley was recorded at Camp Fremont near the campus of Stanford University on September 28, 1918, just four days after the first case was reported in San Francisco. On October 8, the camp imposed a quarantine, and the order was tightened the next day when weekend leaves and Wednesday afternoon liberties were cancelled. Libraries and social halls, set up by service groups to keep soldiers from seeking out bars and brothels, were closed.

In spite of these measures, 8,000 Camp Fremont soldiers in the next six weeks came down with respiratory ailments, and more than 2,400 had to be hospitalized, overwhelming base medical facilities. Although very little was known then about viruses, physicians deduced that this was an airborne disease and began to focus on ventilation. "Men slept with their tent sides rolled up and their bunks alternating head to foot," writes historian Wilcox. Men who had a fever wore masks to the hospital. The cities of San Francisco and Palo Alto put mask orders in place.

The disease was so contagious that on one World War I troop transport, 2,000 of the 9,000 men caught the virus. Of those, 969 had to be hospitalized and 90 died. "The official fatality rate at Camp Fremont," reports author Wilcox, "was 36 percent of pneumonia patients and 5 percent for the epidemic overall."

Forward-thinking scientists urged army doctors to isolate cultures of the virus found in victims and save these specimens for future study. Even though military medical systems were burdened by both a war and a pandemic, some of the physicians at Camp Fremont and elsewhere took the time to do this. In 2005, scientists were able to use two of these cultures taken during military autopsies a century ago to aid in mapping the genome of the 1918 virus. Researchers hope experiments with the genome will one day help prevent future outbreaks.

Camp Fremont was ephemeral. It literally vanished just a few years after the November 11, 1918 armistice, shutting down in April 1920. Its buildings were auctioned off—since in those very different times buildings had more value than land. Among the structures that were sold off and moved: the

Soldiers from Camp Fremont in the Santa Clara Valley, wearing pandemic masks, celebrate the World War I armistice in November 1918 on University Avenue in Palo Alto. *Courtesy Palo Alto Historical Association.*

building that housed the Oasis Beer Garden, a popular watering hole in Menlo Park for sixty years until its closure in 2018. During the brief days of Camp Fremont, the building served as the Camp Fremont YMCA.

But Camp Fremont is still remembered through one man's sacrifice. Harold W. Roberts left the University of California in 1918, trained at Camp Fremont and served overseas in the Meuse-Argonne campaign in an innovative new war weapon called a tank. While the flu raged through his camp back home in California, Roberts was killed in a tank battle during which he gave his life to save the life of his gunner. For his heroism, he was awarded the Medal of Honor. Camp Roberts in Central California is named in his honor.

At the Legion

A recent opinion piece on the opinion-editorial page of the *Wall Street Journal* suggested that veterans' organizations are "fading away" in America. The national commander of the American Legion, Paul E. Dillard, wrote in to the newspaper and begged to differ in a letter to the editor published shortly afterward. The American Legion, he wrote, "remains the largest veterans' organization in the country with more posts in America than Walmart has stores." It has also, he added, had a decisive impact on legislation impacting veterans, including the passage of the Post-9/11 GI Bill. Many people may not know this, but presidential candidates from both parties still regularly speak and campaign at the national conventions of the American Legion.

President Bill Clinton was a delegate to Boys State in Arkansas, and Boys State is an American Legion program. After Clinton was elected governor at his 1963 Boys State Arkansas convention—an election that correctly foreshadowed his later election as the governor of Arkansas—he traveled to Boys Nation in Washington, D.C., where he was not elected president that year but had the chance to meet and be photographed with President John F. Kennedy.

The American Legion post in Los Altos is Post 558, organized in the fall of 1938 at a time when veterans were pondering how to mark the twentieth anniversary of the end of World War I. The post was named for Lieutenant Colonel John J. Howard (1866–1929), whom the old *Los Altos News* called "the most illustrious military citizen Los Altos has ever had." Colonel Howard served in China during the Boxer Rebellion, was badly injured in the Philippine-American War and served as commander of Camp Upton

Left: American Legion Post 558 is named for Lieutenant Colonel John J. Howard, a military hero whose deeds go back to the Boxer Rebellion and the Philippine-American War. After World War I, he retired to Los Altos. *Courtesy American Legion Post 558.*

Below: Veterans of World War I bought the land for American Legion Post 558 in 1940 and built the post themselves on nights and weekends. *Courtesy American Legion Post 558.*

during World War I. After the armistice, he and his wife retired to a house on Robleda Road in Los Altos before his death in 1929.

It wasn't until 1940 that the Legion raised enough money to buy the lot at 347 First Street to begin construction of its building. It is a simple structure built mostly by post members who worked on it nights and weekends and finally got it completed in 1941, just in time for it to serve the community during World War II.

During that second world war of the twentieth century, the Red Cross held classes at the American Legion, and local clubs sponsored dances for service members far from home. No organization involved in World War II support efforts was ever charged a penny for rent by the American Legion.

Los Altos was incorporated late in 1952, and city leaders signed the city charter at the American Legion Hall, which was then the only meeting place of any size within the new city limits. When the old Whitecliff Market burned in 1966—it once occupied the space where Draeger's Market is today—the Legion vacated its building for a year so the store could continue to serve its neighbors.

The building is handmade and plain—a style called Minimal Traditional by architects. But it is old enough now that the post has decided to register the structure as a City Historic Landmark. The land is so valuable in the twenty-first century that the post gets lots of calls from agents who have clients who want to build all kinds of interesting developments on the property. In January 2022, the local Historical Commission unanimously approved Post 558's application for City Landmark status, and members hope this will cut back on the real estate calls.

All service members are taught flag etiquette in the course of their duty, and the veterans of Post 558 have made sharing flag etiquette part of their mission. One of the key elements of this is the respectful retirement of worn and tattered flags. This, in turn, explains the curious red, white and blue box that sits in front of the post.

It looks like a mailbox, and though it is carefully marked "For Deposit of Unserviceable U.S. Flags Only. Not for Mail," people do, from time to time, mistakenly drop in a letter. The good news is that veteran Ken Newman, whose grandfather was an early member of the post and who collects the flags each month from the box, retrieves any stray mail dropped therein and takes it to the post office to send it on its way. But mail isn't all he finds.

"The funniest thing that ends up in that box are rocks. Kids love to open the chute and drop a rock in there," he laughs. "It's okay. I just throw them away."

What happens to the flags? Legion posts throughout the Santa Clara Valley and some Boy Scout troops collect the old flags all year and every June, just before Flag Day, truck hundreds of them to a cemetery in San Jose.

"They get a permit, notify the fire department and we place the flags in two containers and set them ablaze," says United States Marine Corps veteran Mike Welsh, another Post 558 member. "This is the proper way to retire a flag and is done with the utmost respect."

There is no charge for this. It is just one of the many ways veterans continue to serve.

When you meet one—not just on Veterans Day but any day at all—feel free to tip your hat and say, "Thank you for your service."

Chapter 7

AT HOME IN THE VALLEY OF HEART'S DELIGHT

Home is the sailor home from the sea,
And the hunter home from the hill.
—Robert Louis Stevenson

For many in America, home is the place we live before we move to the next place. I left home after graduate school at UCLA and never felt sad about leaving—or so I thought. I loved the adventure of moving to new places. Still, the fact that my parents remained in California in the family home may have served as a kind of safety net for me. The love I felt for the valley where I was born remained.

Moving back to California in 2009 was a revelation. There were stories everywhere I looked—stories I knew about in my region or learned about on my return. To me, they seemed to be asking to be told.

When I sat down to write this next piece, a profile of local historian Don McDonald, whom I mentioned early in this book, I found a man who had started out in California, traveled the world and returned to find himself exactly where he wanted to be—home again.

A CALIFORNIAN AT HOME

Don McDonald, the local historian who authored *Early Los Altos and Los Altos Hills* (Arcadia, 2010) with the Los Altos History Museum, was in his nineties when I was delegated to write a profile of him for the local history

Left: Don McDonald was born in Indiana in 1918. He not only kept the secrets of his work at the NSA, but he also never said a word about his mother putting him in this outfit. *Author's collection.*

Right: Don McDonald at age twelve in Glendale, California, wearing knickerbockers, a popular style for boys then. The palm trees behind him evoke his new home in Southern California in the early twentieth century. *Author's collection.*

quarterly. "Why not wait until I'm a hundred?" he said. "Then we'll really have a story!"

But Don McDonald is so interesting, we saw no reason to wait.

Born in Indiana on July 25, 1918, he moved to Glendale, California, with his family when he was eleven years old. He has now lived through the terms of seventeen U.S. presidents, beginning with Woodrow Wilson. The year he was born, former president Teddy Roosevelt was still making news and America was fighting in World War I. When McDonald's family moved to Glendale, California, Ventura Boulevard was a dirt road. He graduated with the UCLA class of 1940 along with history-making baseball great Jackie Robinson.

A year later, America entered World War II, and McDonald joined up as a naval officer, donning the uniform again in the Korean War. His life has spanned the Jazz Age, the Great Depression, the Space Age, the Atomic Age, the Cold War and, more recently, Silicon Valley and the iPhone. Now, at age ninety-six, he is the paternal head of a clan that includes his three children, seven grandchildren, fifteen great-grandchildren and one great-great-grandchild. A practical man, McDonald has already drafted his obituary.

Of all the inventions he's seen, he says the personal computer is the handiest. You will often find him at his, writing and checking his email. His facility with technology should be no surprise: he had a long career with the highly technical NSA—the National Security Agency—a government agency so secret most Americans didn't know it existed until it was finally written about in the 1970s. McDonald was with the NSA at its founding in 1952 and still says very little about his work.

Much of his NSA cryptology career kept him in the environs of Washington, D.C., but he was also assigned, over the years, to duty stations in Australia and Japan. When he lost his wife in 1969 and subsequently decided to retire, he began to spend more time with friends in California. "I immediately felt I was returning home," he says.

In Los Altos, in 1970, he renewed his acquaintance with Audrey Harper, whom he had met during his college days on a starlit night at the Hollywood Bowl. Audrey married his friend Bob Harper, but by 1970, she, too, was widowed. Though Don loved the cultural advantages of living in the nation's capital, he says, "Audrey made the difference." He drove his VW west and parked it in Los Altos for good. He and Audrey were married, and McDonald returned with ease to being a Californian.

It was his walks through the remnants of the apricot orchards near their home that sparked his interest in local history. He was one of the first docents at the J. Gilbert Smith House in 1978, and there, on quiet afternoons, his curiosity and his long career collecting and analyzing data led him to the newspaper files in the basement. He uncovered so much that the research led to a popular series of history columns he penned for the *Los Altos Town Crier* and to his book.

Lieutenant JG Don McDonald in 1943 when he served in the U.S. Navy during World War II. His navy work involved cryptography, which became the work of his career. *Author's collection.*

He became a local preservationist and was one of the first to stand up for the Los Altos Heritage Orchard when there were plans for a new civic center on the site. "I'm appalled to see the orchard getting the short end of the stick," he told a local reporter in the year 2000, as he posed for a photograph among the apricot trees. He was then serving on the Historical Commission, and his voice made a difference; other residents joined him and together worked to defend the Heritage Orchard, which still stands.

McDonald continues to be interested in history, but his interests range far beyond that. In addition to his code-breaking career and his writing, he has traveled the world, taught poetry, trod the boards in amateur theater, played classical piano and studied oil painting. Among many other activities, he served as president of the Peninsula Civil War Round Table and has been an active member of a slew of other groups, from the Peninsula Astronomical Society, to the Navy Cryptologic Veterans Association, to the uniquely Californian society called E Clampus Vitus—which is a sort of drinking society for history buffs. Or a history society for drinking buffs. (He says it depends on the chapter.)

He quips that he belongs in "a rest home for the chronically inquisitive" and admits he would love to enjoy many more birthdays, "as long as I can keep all my marbles." This summer, he stopped by to enjoy the annual volunteer party at the Los Altos History Museum, marking his thirty-sixth year as a member. Later, sitting in the sunlight of the Los Altos home he and Audrey share, he asks: "Is there any place nicer than this?" Since there's no need for an answer, Don McDonald, who is now headed toward birthday number ninety-seven, simply smiles.

This profile was published in 2014. Don died in Los Altos three years later, just shy of his ninety-ninth birthday.

HOME AND A HOBBY

For some of us, the origin of our passions goes back to the things we loved most in the homes of our childhoods. This story is about a Santa Clara Valley man who loved his family home so much that he can no longer drive by it now that his parents are gone and it has been sold. Long before that, when his parents were still living in Los Altos Hills and he was making a new home for himself in Danville, California, he called his folks and arranged to take a piece of his childhood across the bay to Danville.

It all has to do with a train set. And, full disclosure, I must tell you that I have known the hero of this story nearly all of my life.

Alden Huling Woodworth Andersen—always known as "Stretch"—was raised in a house on Miranda Court in the Santa Clara Valley foothills with a sweeping view of San Francisco Bay. Although his father was the art director at Stanford Research Institute, Ray Andersen and his wife, Judy, had been, in an earlier chapter of their lives, a professional ballroom dance team. In fact, many residents of the valley today remember taking lessons in ballroom dancing from the Andersens in the studio they built over their garage.

One Christmas Eve, Stretch's father brought home a model train made by Märklin, a German company. Stretch traces his love of European trains to that moment. "I knew my train was different from the American ones owned by my friends," he says today. "And I guess I liked that."

He packed away his engines and track when he attended Los Altos High School. Model trains were not very cool for high school students back then. Stretch was a leader at LAHS and served in the student senate, then as president of his class and finally as president of the student body.

Santa Clara Valley native Stretch Andersen and his European model trains are known throughout the San Francisco Bay Area and beyond. *Photo by Michelle Andersen.*

After he graduated from Santa Clara University and bought his first home in Danville, Stretch asked his folks to dig out the Märklin trains so he could put them under his Christmas tree. When he married and had a family of his own, he joined a national group called the European Train Enthusiasts (ETE). And when he and his wife and daughter moved to a larger house in Danville, his wife, Michelle, claims she had an inkling that Stretch wanted the extra space for his trains.

Was she right? All we can say is that like his parents, Stretch eventually added a room over the garage to accommodate his avocation.

As he reached his sixties, Stretch decided to retire. This gave him time to join the national board of ETE and become, over time, its treasurer, webmaster and editor of its quarterly journal. He has now organized ETE exhibits all over the San Francisco Bay Area at, among other venues, the Hiller Aviation Museum, Oakland Aviation Museum, Blackhawk Museum and the Maker Faire at the San Mateo County Events Center. With the help of his wife, he has used these events to raise money for various charities, including the U.S. Marine Corps' Toys for Tots campaign and the Danville-based Crayon Initiative.

During the Covid-19 pandemic, when everybody was stuck at home for months and feeling gloomy, Stretch found in this yet another opportunity. He electronically expanded his network of train enthusiasts beyond the Bay Area, and beyond California, to begin a series of both national and international Zoom webinars with ETE members. They shared ideas from Berkeley to Brookline to Berlin. Stretch, who has never been shy, became an international ETE Zoom celebrity.

With so many people in Silicon Valley obsessed with work, you might find it refreshing to find a man obsessed with 1:87 scale model European trains and the miniature landscapes through which they travel.

There is a certain magic to this lifelong passion, since it all began at the home a boy loved in the hills above the Valley of Heart's Delight one Christmas Eve.

You Can Go Home Again; or the Case of the Two Ronald Reagans

I had two childhood homes, and they were conveniently located across the street from one another. The first is the one my father built on weekends after World War II on what was then called Clark Avenue.

My father loved beautiful cars. But he was so thrifty he only talked himself into buying one new car in his whole life. This is it, a 1959 Oldsmobile 88, so long it appears to be taking up most of our driveway. *Author's collection.*

Looking back, I recall having a great affection for that handmade house. Ten years later, after Clark Avenue had changed its name to Echo Drive, we moved across the street into our second family home. The move was so convenient, we only had to hire movers to carry grandmother's grand piano across the street.

The new place was bigger and more sophisticated and had the luxury of two bathrooms. But I never felt as warm toward the second house as I did toward the first. And yet, when my parents died in this second home, I had a terrible time letting it go. I moved in, temporarily, and eight years later, I was still there.

There were many advantages to living in an old family home. It had a connection to family history, of course, and ours was in a beautiful community. There are disadvantages too. My late parents had exacting standards, and sometimes, when I was busy writing and let the weeds grow in the garden, I could feel their disapproval as they frowned down upon me from the great beyond.

It was this fear of their astral dismay that drove me, after about six or seven years of procrastination, to climb up into the crawl space above the garage and finally go through several old cardboard boxes up there. For approximately three decades before she died, my mother had asked me to sort through them and, please, get them out of her way. Like many young people, I thought of my parents as the conservators of my childhood. It seemed churlish of them to thrust these memories back at me.

Especially so since this is exactly the kind of task many of us avoid. What does one do with the stuff? It included the usual scrapbooks, athletic awards, academic paperwork and valentines from a long way back.

Once I got started, it wasn't too bad. I uncovered some photos I took at an August 1962 San Francisco Giants game at Candlestick Park of a St. Louis

St. Louis Cardinals player Bill White in two photos I snapped of him at Candlestick Park in the 1960s. In 1989, White became the first African American president of the National League. Future hall of famers Willie Mays and Willie McCovey also played at Candlestick Park that day, but I didn't get a chance to take their pictures. *Photos by Robin Chapman.*

Cardinal who came over to the fence and talked to some of us kids before the game. After so many years, I didn't recognize him, but I looked up his number and discovered he was (and is) Bill White, born in 1934, who in 1989 became the first African American president of the National League. He played a short time for the Giants, which explains why the kids near me had been calling him over to the fence. The Giants had a great roster in those days, including future hall of famers Willie Mays and Willie McCovey, but they didn't stroll into camera range. Since my thrifty father bought the tickets, we were in the bleacher seats with the rest of the peanut gallery.

When I reached the layer from 1964, I slowed down. My parents were active in the GOP in those days, and my father took the entire family to the Cow Palace several times that summer to attend the Republican National Convention. Sorting through the box, I recalled the day we drove up to the city where we hoped to catch a glimpse of the Republican presidential nominee as he left the St. Francis Hotel to head for the convention and give his acceptance speech.

There was no traffic to speak of, and we found a parking spot with ease. That's how long ago it was.

If you know your history, you know Barry Goldwater's 1964 presidential race ended in defeat. But among the memorabilia in the box, I found something I acquired the day we spent hanging around the lobby of the St. Francis. It was an autograph I got from a man who was famous then but became even more famous later.

I had completely forgotten about it until I came across it. It is an autograph scrawled on the back of an envelope, and when I saw it, the scene came back to me:

A man steps into the hotel lobby from the elevator. My mother nudges me with her elbow and says, "That's Ronald Reagan. See if you can get his autograph!" My father reaches into the inside pocket of his sports coat, finds an envelope and hands it to me. All this takes seconds, and then, as if in slow motion, I take the envelope, turn it to the blank side, walk over to Mr. Reagan and request an autograph. He smiles, pulls out a fountain pen and signs. Fade out.

Though I later covered President Reagan when he served in the White House, that day in 1964 when I first laid eyes on him, I did not know anything about his politics. I recognized him as the sometime host of the TV program *Death Valley Days*.

Presidential autographs are valuable, and their provenance is important. Once a leader in America reaches the Oval Office, much of his correspondence is signed by something called the Autopen, which copies the president's signature for him. Thus, a pre-Autopen autograph still in the possession of the original autograph hound is a keeper. The provenance is excellent, and this one celebrates the coincidence of the child later becoming a reporter who covered the man who later became president.

And that is not the end of the coincidences. Nor the end of my finds.

The Ronald Reagan autograph I got from the future president in San Francisco. *Photo by Robin Chapman.*

After I first published this story in 2018, I went through another box at the old homestead and found something from the summer I was a delegate to Girls State in Sacramento, the leadership program I mentioned in a previous chapter. You may recall that Bill Clinton was elected governor when he was a delegate to Arkansas Boys State and thus got to go to Washington, D.C., to meet President John F. Kennedy.

Nothing quite that exciting happened to me in Sacramento. At least not that I remembered. But when I went through that second box, I found something surprising: a second Ronald Reagan autograph. I had completely forgotten about this one, too.

Once again, as I looked at the artifact, the story came back:

We were on a Girls State tour of the capitol when then-governor Ronald Reagan stepped out of a private door and greeted us in the hallway. Me, the future reporter, grabbed the nearest piece of paper at hand and asked, as had apparently become my custom, for his autograph. He smiled (again), pulled out a pen and signed my piece of paper. With apologies to the Founding Fathers, it was the Preamble to the Constitution, part of my Girls State packet.

What astonishes me today is that when I covered President Reagan, I didn't remember any of this. Journalists, it is true, live in the present. Perhaps in my mind, I had left my past behind. And anyway, no journalist would ever ask the president of the United States for an autograph. Possibly, I blotted it all out in my shame. Possibly, I did remember and just figured nobody would believe me. If I didn't have these two autographs now, I would hardly believe it myself.

The Ronald Reagan autograph I got a few years later in Sacramento. *Photo by Robin Chapman.*

It certainly is a reminder of several things. Don't throw away old stuff in your family home before you go through it. Also: childhood really is a place we demonstrate the passions that lead us into the future. Also: life is full of coincidences. And finally: many of us, even in a country as large as ours, are closer than even six degrees of separation from the White House.

Afterword

HOME AGAIN

*I*f it is true that life is what happens to us while we are planning other things, then my return to California to care for my aging parents in 2009 is confirmation of that. After both my parents died, the house they left behind became a treasure-trove of clues to both regional history and family tales.

I learned my paternal grandfather had served in World War I, something I may have heard but have since learned a great deal more about from family papers. I was able to link his service to a better understanding of the Santa Clara Valley's Camp Fremont and the 1918 pandemic. I discovered my father's letters to my mother from World War II in an old footlocker. It was a collection so personal and so emotional for me, I have been unable to find a way to share it with the public. Yet those letters are part of a global story of war and of the great change war brings, and it remains a story I hope one day to tell.

I found a drawer in a bureau filled with a small array of things my maternal grandmother left behind when she died, including an unfinished piece of lace tatting still attached to a spool. Since I never saw my grandmother making lace, I wondered if she had been working on that, or was it something her own mother, born in Holland, had left behind? Objects that speak of the lives of many generations of my family filled that old house. Each one contained a story that linked my family's story to the history of our community and our country. Do you recall the museum curator I interviewed who spoke of the power of objects? "It is a magical thing to encounter an object a century old," she said. "Something really special happens between object and viewer." That is the absolute truth. It is hard to understand history from the dry dates of eras. History is the story of people. How my double-great-grandmother reacted to the Crow Indian man. How that unfinished piece of lace links my grandmother to her immigrant past.

How fragile we are. How lucky I was to find these little pieces of magic and then to share them. The writer Amy Tan says writers often write about one subject and learn, in fact, they have produced "unintended memoirs." The writer's subconscious is a powerful thing.

Not so very long after I wrote that article about home and sorting through the boxes there, I looked around and realized I did not want to spend the rest of my life in a house I had always thought of as belonging to my late parents. I had begun to wonder if I was still hanging around because I hoped to somehow rewrite the story there. Perhaps there was another reason I had not yet acknowledged.

In any case, my head knew it was time to close out the last details of the family estate and find myself a new place. It was a sensible decision, though much more difficult than I imagined. Newton's first law is always a barrier, i.e. things in motion tend to stay in motion and things at rest to stay at rest. Yet somehow, I knew it was time to go.

That decision precipitated one of the most difficult periods of my life. My extended family is scattered across America, so I faced the tasks alone. It was never, of course, entirely about the material things in the house. What was new was the ache in my heart. It has taken me until just as I write this to understand that my heart—as a friend pointed out during my move—had simply not caught up with my head.

When we do jobs like this after the deaths of people we love, we are sorting through the remains of their lives and sorting through, as well, so many of the symbols of our relationships with them. We find things that speak of their habits, their hobbies and, perhaps, of important moments of intimacy we shared. Or intimacy we longed for and never shared. Doing this, we confront our own mortality. One day, someone will be doing this for us.

In my case, it felt as if everything that could possibly go wrong did go wrong. My to-do list was so long, I began to dream about it the way I used to dream about being late and unprepared for final exams at school. Then the pandemic arrived. The stock market fell. I hesitated to say things couldn't get worse for fear I might be wrong and they would.

The pandemic removed resources I depended on: church, gym and library closed. The organizations to which I belonged, with their lectures, collegial

The front page of the *San Jose Mercury*, July 21, 1969. It is one of the many pieces of history I saved long ago and rediscovered in a cardboard box in my family home. *Author's collection.*

gatherings and laughter, vanished like Brigadoon. I didn't just *feel* isolated; I was. But, of course, so was the rest of the country.

I began to notice that experiencing stress is one of the worst things a person can do to her body, and my health took a beating. In desperation, I began to walk several miles a day. I didn't have to wear a mask when I was outside, and I saw other people also out walking and we waved, furtively, as our paths crossed. It was a healthy decision, and I walked off some of the turmoil.

The work got done. The family archive was sorted, donated, recycled, scanned, curb surfed, sold, tossed, hauled away and stored—though reviewing it all, touching it all was difficult, day after day. Eventually, the family kitchen got its new coat of paint. The baths got new fixtures.

Once tuned up, the house sold quickly. Now into temporary digs (several) with boxes in storage. Challenging. And now: where to go?

When I was young, on hot summer weekends in the valley when the family chores were done, we used to drive over to the beach near Half Moon Bay. We packed a picnic, put our swimsuits on under our clothes, piled into the Chevrolet and headed over the hills. Summer can be the coldest season in the environs of the California coast, and the photos we snapped often show us shivering by the sea. But you could still gather driftwood then and build a fire, so we would do that and warm ourselves and roast our marshmallows before we piled back into the Chevy to head for home. I have always loved the coast. After our family home sold in the valley, I began to look for something I liked near the ocean.

Seven months later, just as I was about to give up, I found a place on a hill just a short walk from the Pacific. I made an offer and was surprised to find myself a homeowner again. I gave the interior a coat of paint, replaced a couple of light fixtures, refinished the living room floor and moved in—my fourth address in eleven months. The bedroom has a view of the ocean, and the garden is filled with pots of flowers and succulents in a climate where agapanthus bloom year-round and finicky hydrangeas love the blend of seaside light and shade. On my walks, I even spotted two apricot trees in two different neighbors' gardens.

The first afternoon in the new house, I heard the call of an owl in the backyard, and after that, I heard him almost every day. I looked up the call and identified the visitor as a burrowing owl, though he was shy and I never did catch a glimpse of him. The ancients viewed the appearance of an owl as a good omen. I was more than willing to agree.

Then, one evening, I heard a sound so loud outside my bedroom window I thought a large dog was barking. Fearing this might mean trouble, I opened

My father and me on the beach near Half Moon Bay, a long time ago. I look pretty cold, but the photo still makes me smile. *Author's collection.*

my upstairs sliding door and stepped out onto the balcony. I heard the sound of a sea lion barking at the beach not far away; but that wasn't what had brought me outside. The foghorn blared, but that wasn't it either. After a minute, I heard the deep and resounding call of a great horned owl, and I stood, listening. When he called again, I spotted him perched in a nearby pine. I had found one of his feathers in my driveway the week before, and his appearance, to me, signaled a double owl omen for my new home. Like two full moons in a month or two apricot trees in the neighborhood, it seemed to me this had primitive implications of a rich and auspicious time. At a minimum, it meant good birdwatching.

"They say the day you die your name is written on a cloud," says a character in the noir classic *Out of the Past*. Who says that, I wonder? I love

141

these old adages. I do believe there are signs of which we can catch glimpses from time to time that will cheer us on our way. If the Valley of Heart's Delight is a sort of mystical place we can't quite touch, it is good to have that in one's life. Our life is shaped by so much more than our conscious will. And until that day one's name is written on a cloud, everything we do and every place we live is always subject to change.

I remain a Californian with a home in my home state, just a slightly more rural twenty-nine miles from the Santa Clara Valley and the friends I love. A family bought our old home, and it needed a family to share its gardens and to make new memories. I wish them happiness.

I have a new home where boxes of scrapbooks no longer call to me. Where I no longer hear the echo of my father's long-legged stride as he heads up the street from the old train station in the twilight. My father might have been growing tired of all those walks he had been taking in my mind and heart. And tired as well of that flight over the Santa Cruz Mountains where he accidentally gave himself the hot seat. Maybe he'll never grow tired of reliving the moment he handed me the envelope I handed to Ronald Reagan, who signed it with his fountain pen on that day in San Francisco. When you think about it, to an old trooper like Reagan, my father, mother and I were just what the script called for when we came in right on cue. I, the budding journalist, liked the part so much I took it on the road to Sacramento and on into the rest of my life.

Why was leaving that old house so tough? I have thought about this quite a bit now that I'm resettled, and I still know only part of the answer. It was the end of something, and I may not have been ready for that. Novelist Gabrielle Zevin says, "All stories…are attempts to explain the world to one another and for ourselves." Clearly my writing of history's stories is part of a larger effort to understand my family and my place in it. That's the most I know for the present.

Now I am in a community with new stories and in a home where ghosts no longer haunt the halls. It doesn't mean I can't conjure them up when necessary. The difference is that now, in my new surroundings, these spirits no longer dictate the time and place.

Meanwhile, I am back at work by the Pacific as the owls call out on the breeze.

ACKNOWLEDGEMENTS

A writer and journalist must write for publication in order to stay useful and in tune—kind of like an old piano. Thus, this book would not have been possible if I had not had regular platforms for the stories I began to research and write when I returned to California. The primary outlet for my work has been the *Los Altos Town Crier*, and for this I owe a great debt to the late *LATC* publisher Paul Nyberg, his wife and business partner, Liz, the present publishers and the always upbeat editor-in-chief, Bruce Barton.

Thanks to the Los Altos History Museum for using some of my earliest pieces in the museum's quarterly publication, *Under the Oaks*. The former director there was one of the first people I met at the museum, and she was among the first to enlist me as a writer. And by the way, without the help of the present museum board and staff, we may have had to wait several more years to get that sign in the Los Altos Heritage Orchard, so a very big note of thanks to all involved in that. Annette Stransky, president of the Saratoga Historical Foundation and editor of the foundation's quarterly newsletter, has also published my articles, hosted book talks for me and included me in the Saratoga Blossom Festival. It was at one of her events that I learned the history of the electric interurban railroads in a talk by historian Ray Cosyn, and Ray helped me research my first article on these interurban lines.

Alex Atkins, who edits *Our Town* in Los Altos Hills, was another who asked me to write for him. With his help, I researched a series on Juana Briones and wrote my first piece on Wallace Stegner—both of which I drew on for this book. Thanks to Lynn Stegner for pointing me to the archives of the Marriott Library in Utah, where I was able to uncover some excellent images of her late father-in-law.

One of the many local archives I have relied on is History San José. Cate Mills is the dedicated archivist there, and San Jose and the rest of us are lucky she is. Brian George at the Palo Alto Historical Association (PAHA) has been a great help to me over the years on images. Also, Palo Alto historian Steve Staiger at PAHA has a whole archive in his cranium; I have relied on that as well. Speaking of Palo Alto, several years after I perused the archives of the old *Palo Alto Times* at the City of Palo Alto Library regarding the 1954 visit of Frank Lloyd Wright, I found reference librarian Kasper Kimura especially kind. I had the dates of the articles and the data but needed the exact headlines for my bibliography. She ran them down for me and saved me using some of those expensive fossil fuels to drive over to Palo Alto.

Early in my career, I worked with San Francisco native Rick Laubscher in the KRON-TV newsroom and found him to be a fellow history buff. I remember one day, especially, when we talked about biographies of Jack London. Move forward into the twenty-first century, and Rick is now serving as president and CEO of the Market Street Railway in San Francisco, an independent nonprofit focused on preserving the historic transit of San Francisco. It was to Rick I turned when I pondered how, in August 1879, Robert Louis Stevenson would have made the journey from San Francisco to Monterey. Rick put me in touch with volunteer Emiliano Echevveria at the Market Street Railway for the help I needed. The California State Railroad Museum also assisted on that story and several others.

The Robert Louis Stevenson Club of Monterey was the first to request an article on my research into the life of Dorothy Emily Stevenson, and I thank longtime club official Lindy Perez for that. Mitchell Manson, geneticist and president of the RLS Club of Edinburgh, reviewed my draft, gave me information on the DNA of writer cousins and then requested the article for his *RLS Club News* in Scotland. The Monterey club commissioned the article, but the Edinburgh club published it first—and there were smiles all around, so that was great. Then, in May 2021, again with the help of Mitchell Manson, my article on DES appeared in a French RLS club publication— my first article on the Continent. I am very grateful to all the RLS clubs involved for making my RLS and DES discoveries so much fun.

Thanks to Dr. Carol Lynn McKibben of Stanford University for her help on discriminatory covenants in twentieth-century California real estate deeds and in America at the end of World War II. I am indebted to writer

Jan Batiste Adkins, who was a thoughtful source and friend as I worked on that story. Herb and Diana Parsons of the Moffett Historical Society and Museum have been guides over the years to the many stories at Moffett Field. They have dedicated much of their lives to preserving the military history of our region, specifically the history of Naval Air Station Moffett, and I'm indebted to both of them for their input on this book. Ken Newman of American Legion Post 558 not only helped me long ago repair the halyard on the flagpole at my family home, but he also let me know about his post's plan to seek landmark status for its building and did the research that made my stories on that possible.

These sources and friends and many more besides have been there to help me uncover the true tales of the Valley of Heart's Delight. The ride has been much enhanced by their company.

SELECTED BIBLIOGRAPHY

Ackroyd, Peter. *Alfred Hitchcock: A Brief Life*. New York: Doubleday, 2015.

Adkins, Jan Batiste. *African Americans of San Jose and Santa Clara County*. Charleston, SC: Arcadia Publishing, 2019.

Arbuckle, Clyde, and Ralph Rambo. *Santa Clara County Ranchos*. San Jose, CA: Rosicrucian Press, 1968.

Balls, Edward K. *Early Uses of California Plants*. Berkeley: University of California Press, 1962.

Bancroft, H.H. *California Pioneer Register and Index, 1542–1848: Including Inhabitants of California, 1769–1800, and List of Pioneers*. Baltimore: Regional Publishing Company, 1964.

Beebe, Rose Marie, and Robert M. Senkewicz. *Lands of Promise and Despair: Chronicles of Early California, 1535–1846*. Berkeley: Heyday Books, 2001.

Benson, Jackson. *Wallace Stegner: His Life and Work*. New York: Viking, 1996.

Big Timber Pioneer. "Dusting Off the Old Ones." February 11, 1926. Includes details on the life of Luthena Brumfield.

"Bing Crosby Rediscovered." PBS *American Masters*, first aired December 2, 2014. Directed by Robert Trachtenberg. DVD: 1 hour and 25 minutes.

Bland, Henry Meade. *Stevenson's California*. San Jose, CA: Pacific Short Story Club, 1924.

Brilliant, Mark. *The Color of America Has Changed: How Racial Diversity Shaped Civil Rights Reform in California, 1941–1978*. Oxford, UK: Oxford University Press, 2010.

Chapman, Robin. *California Apricots: The Lost Orchards of Silicon Valley*. Charleston, SC: The History Press, 2013.

———. *Historic Bay Area Visionaries*. Charleston, SC: The History Press, 2018.

Consigny, Jean Marie. "Four California Gardens." *California History Nugget* 5, no. 3. California State Historical Association, December 1937.

DeRooy, Carola. Archivist and museum program manager, Point Reyes National Seashore. Telephone interview and email communications with the author on the donated photograph believed to be Juana Briones, October 2017.

Dillard, Paul E. "The American Legion Isn't Going Anywhere." *Wall Street Journal*, September 28, 2021, Letters to the Editor.

du Maurier, Daphne. *The Birds and Other Stories*. London: Virago Press, Little Brown Book Group, 2004.

Fradkin, Philip L. *Wallace Stegner and the American West*. New York: Alfred A. Knopf, 2008.

Gennis, Rita. *Lots of 'Cots: Cooking with Apricots*. Carmichael, CA: Ben Ali Books, 1989.

Giddins, Gary. *Bing Crosby, a Pocketful of Dreams: The Early Years 1903–1940*. New York: Back Bay Books, 2009.

———. *Bing Crosby, Swinging on a Star: The War Years, 1940–1946*. New York: Little, Brown and Company, 2018.

Hackel, Steven W. *Junípero Serra: California's Founding Father*. New York: Hill & Wang, 2013.

Haworth, Elia. Curator of Marin Art and History, Bolinas Museum, Bolinas, CA. Telephone interview and email communications with the author, January 2022.

Hilton, George W., and John F. Due. *The Electric Interurban Railways in America*. Stanford: Stanford University Press, 1960.

Hom, Gloria Sun, ed. *Chinese Argonauts: An Anthology of the Chinese Contributions in the Historical Development of Santa Clara County*. Los Altos Hills: California History Center, 1971.

Hoover, Mildred Brook, Hero Eugene Rensch and Ethel Grace Rensch. *Historic Spots in California*. Stanford, CA: Stanford University Press, 1948 and 1990 editions.

Huestis, Lyle. W. "Apples of Gold in Settings of Silver." Los Altos History Museum archives, unpublished memoir, 1977.

Hutchings, Robin. "Pioneer Home Which Will House Los Altos History Will Be Dedicated on City Birthday." *Los Altos Town Crier*, November 30, 1977.

Ignoffo, Mary Jo. *Captive of the Labyrinth: Sarah L. Winchester Heiress to the Rifle Fortune*. Columbia, MO: University of Missouri Press, 2010.

Irvine, Leigh. *Santa Clara County, California: "The Valley of Heart's Delight."* Published by the Board of Supervisors of Santa Clara County, CA, 1914. Reprint, 2009.

Jacobson, Yvonne Olson. *Passing Farms, Enduring Values: California's Santa Clara Valley.* Los Altos: William Kaufmann, Inc., 1984.

Kimbro, Edna E., and Julia G. Costello. *The California Missions: History, Art and Preservation.* Los Angeles: Getty Conservation Institute, 2009.

Kolstad, John. Telephone interviews with the author regarding the California Bell Company, January and February 2019 and October 15, 2021.

Kurillo, Max, and Erline Tuttle. *A Guide to the Historic Bells of Mrs. A.S.C. Forbes.* Self-published by John Kolstad, 2004.

Lane, L.W. "Bill," Jr. *The Sun Never Sets: Reflections on a Western Life.* Stanford, CA: Stanford General Books, 2013.

Los Altos News. "Bing Says 'Yes' to Invitation to Youth Center Dedication." January 5, 1961.

———. "City Studies Youth Center Use Priority." September 8, 1960.

———. "City to Buy Furnishings for Youth Center." September 15, 1960.

———. "Dancers and Painters Took Over Los Altos Youth Center This Week." Photo essay, October 13, 1960.

———. "Dedication Set for Youth Center." January 12, 1961.

———. "Formal Opening of Youth Center Is Proposed." October 20, 1960.

———. "House Tour to Benefit Los Altos Youth Center." September 22, 1960.

———. "The LAYC—'A Dream Come True,'" and photo essay, "Mayors Show Crosby Plaque: Bing Not There to Receive It." January 19, 1961.

———. "New Los Altos Youth Center May Be Opened Next Week." October 4, 1960.

———. "Noted Artist Helps Prepare for Dedication." January 12, 1961.

———. "Singer, Golf Stars Here Jan. 15." January 5, 1961.

———. "Youth Center Dedication Planned Jan. 8." November 3, 1960.

Los Altos Town Crier. "Dedication Set for Youth Center." January 11, 1961.

Margolin, Malcolm. *The Ohlone Way: Indian Life in the San Francisco–Monterey Bay Area.* Berkeley: Heyday, 1978.

Mattson, Phyllis Helene. *War Orphan in San Francisco: Letters Link a Family Scattered by World War II.* Cupertino: Stevens Creek Press, 2005.

McDonald, Don, and the Los Altos History Museum. *Early Los Altos and Los Altos Hills.* Charleston, SC: Arcadia Publishing, 2010.

McDonnell, Jeanne Farr. *Juana Briones of Nineteenth-Century California.* Tucson: University of Arizona Press, 2008.

McGilligan, Patrick. *Alfred Hitchcock: A Life in Darkness and Light*. New York: Regan Books/HarperCollins, 2003.

McKevitt, Gerald, SJ. *The University of Santa Clara: A History, 1851–1977*. Palo Alto: Stanford University Press, 1979.

Newman, Kenneth. Telephone interviews with the author regarding Los Altos American Legion Post 558, October 2018 and February 2020.

Nickerson, Roy. *Robert Louis Stevenson in California: A Remarkable Courtship*. San Francisco: Chronicle Books, 1982.

Nyberg, Paul D. *Los Altos: Portrait of a Community, a Century of Photographs*. Los Altos: Select Books, 1992.

Olson, Charles. Telephone and in-person interviews with the author regarding Dave Packard of Hewlett-Packard and their friendship, May 2018.

Oshinsky, David. "The Long History of Vaccine Mandates in America." *Wall Street Journal*, September 18–19, 2021, C1–C2.

Palo Alto Times. "Architect Frank L. Wright to Speak at Stanford Tonight." February 10, 1954.

Parsons, Diana. Telephone and in-person interviews with the author regarding the Moffett Historical Society Museum collection of sweetheart military jewelry, January 2018.

Parsons, Harry "Herb." Telephone interviews with the author regarding Rear Admiral William A. Moffett, his Medal of Honor and ceremonial sword, May 2018.

Parsons, Mary Elizabeth. *The Wild Flowers of California: Their Names, Haunts and Habits*. San Francisco: California Academy of Sciences, 1955. First published in 1897.

Rothstein, Richard. *The Color of Law: The Forgotten History of How Our Government Segregated America*. New York: W.W. Norton/Liveright, 2017.

Rousch, Colonel John H. Roush, Jr., ed. *World War II Reminiscences: A Collection of Vivid Memories of Combat during World War II*. Kentfield: Reserve Officers Association of the United States, California Department, 1995 and 1996.

San Jose Business Journal. "From Farms to Fabs: 100 Years of Business in the Valley." December 24, 1999.

San Jose Mercury Herald. "Funeral Rites for Thos. Chew to Be Delayed." February 25, 1931, 3.

Santa Cruz Sentinel. "Alfred Hitchcock Using *Sentinel*'s Seabird Story." August 21, 1961, 1.

———. "Seabird Invasion Hits Coastal Homes." August 18, 1961, 1.

Sawyer, Eugene T. *History of Santa Clara County, California*. Los Angeles: Historic Record Company, 1922.

Shattock, James. Interview and electronic communication with the author regarding Bing Crosby plaque and photograph, February–April 2020.

Shepherd, Doris "Tuck." "Oldtimers Recall Los Altos' Past." *Los Altos Town Crier*, July 8, 1981.

Shoup, Laurence H., Randall T. Milliken and Alan K. Brown. "Inigo of Rancho Posolmi: The Life and Times of a Mission Indian and His Land." Unpublished report for Tasman Corridor Archaeological Project, Santa Clara County Transportation Agency. Archaeological/Historical Consultants for Woodward-Clyde Consultants, Oakland, California. May 1995. History San José Archives.

Stallings, Bud. "Sunday Is the Big Day! Teen Center Dedication." *Los Altos News*, January 12, 1961.

Stanford Daily. "Frank Lloyd Wright to Lecture Tonight," February 10, 1954.

———. "Frank Lloyd Wright to Speak." February 8, 1954.

Starrs, Paul F., and Peter Goin. *Field Guide to California Agriculture*. Berkeley: University of California Press, 2010.

Stegner, Wallace Earle. *All the Little Live Things*. New York: Viking Press, 1967.

Stevenson, Robert Louis. *The Travels and Essays of Robert Louis Stevenson: The Amateur Emigrant, Across the Plains, the Silverado Squatters*. New York: Charles Scribner's Sons, 1911.

Taaffe, Linda. "Proposed Civic Center Could Replace Historic Orchard at Los Altos City Hall." *Los Altos Town Crier*, October 4, 2000.

Terry, R.C. *Robert Louis Stevenson: Interviews and Recollections*. London: Macmillan Press Ltd., 1996.

Todd, Geraldine. "Architecture of Future to Express Freedom of Democracy 'in True Sense' Says Wright." *Palo Alto Times*, February 11, 1954.

Trabing, Wally. "Thousands of Birds Floundering in Streets." *Santa Cruz Sentinel*, August 21, 1961.

White, Frank. Telephone and in-person interviews with the author regarding his childhood in Los Altos during the years 1940–50, August 2018.

Wickson, Edward J. *The California Fruits and How to Grow Them*. San Francisco: Pacific Rural Press, 1914 and 1926.

———. *Rural California*. New York: Macmillan Company, 1923.

Wilcox, Barbara. *World War I Army Training by San Francisco Bay: The Story of Camp Fremont*. Charleston, SC: The History Press, 2016.

Williams, Esther, and Digby Diehl. *The Million Dollar Mermaid: An Autobiography*. New York: Simon & Schuster, 1999.

INDEX